HOFFA!

Ten Angels Swearing

AN

AUTHORIZED

BIOGRAPHY

BY

JIM CLAY

BEAVERDAM BOOKS, INC.
Beaverdam, Virginia

Hoffa . . . Ten Angels Swearing

Preface and Dedication

Before the bar of justice the accused stands innocent, at least in theory, until or unless proved guilty by due process of law. Thus he may present evidence on his own behalf, call witnesses to testify for him, refute evidence against him, and cross examine hostile witnesses. And he has the right of appeal.

No such principle or theory exists to protect a man on trial in the court of public opinion. The principle of "free press" has no practical application to help him. There is no due process. Thus he may be utterly destroyed in the public's eye, however unjustly, and he is virtually powerless to fight back. Usually in such cases a man's "public image" is devastated before he is aware of what has happened to him. It's like being talked about behind your back on a very large scale. Rumor, if repeated often enough and especially if put into print, becomes truth.

In the legal world Edward Bennett Williams is the outstanding, modern exponent of the principle of innocence and equality before the law and due process even for the damned. He has defended many unpopular and controversial persons, including James R. Hoffa. In writing this, an authorized biography which presents the good things about Mr. Hoffa as well as his own point of view on some bad things, I have extended the principle to the world of publicity and public relations.

My book is dedicated to Edward Bennett Williams whose own eloquent appeal for justice, *One Man's Freedom*, ought to be read by everyone.

JAMES CLAY

CONTENTS

CHAPTER 1

Who Is The Real Jimmy Hoffa?

THIS book has been stirring around in my mind for several years. It began in 1958 when my agent telephoned from New York to ask me to ghost-write an article about Jimmy Hoffa. It went without saying that this was supposed to relate in summary the sensational things that had been reported in countless news stories as the result of Senate committee investigations and public hearings. It did not occur to me that any other type of story could be written about Jimmy Hoffa. All I knew was what I had seen and heard through the news media.

My first thought was to collect several routine Hoffa articles (newspapers and magazines had been full of them for months); pull from them choice bits; do a little paraphasing and there would be my piece. This is called research-writing and it saves a lot of leg and brain work.

All Hoffa stories of the time were pretty much the same. They consisted mainly of material lifted from press releases handed out by the Senate Select Committee on Improper Activities in the Labor and/or Management Field; the McClellan Committee.

Chief Counsel of the Committee, in charge of investigations, public hearings, and press releases, was Robert F. Kennedy.

The articles about Jim Hoffa and the hearings were so repetitious and stereotyped that I decided to break the first rule of a lazy writer (which I am) and do original research. To begin with, I put together a brief biographical sketch of my subject; James Riddle Hoffa.

He was born on February 14, 1913, at Brazil, Indiana. His father was John Hoffa, a driller for a coal prospector. His mother was Viola Riddle, a pretty Irish girl. There were four children; two girls and two boys.

Jimmy was seven when his father died.

In 1922 Mrs. Hoffa moved the family to Clinton, Indiana. It is said that she took in washing.

Jimmy went to school until he was fourteen, finishing the ninth grade. He quit to help support the family. His first job was as a stock boy in a dry goods store. He stayed on for a year and a half, with no pay raises in the meantime.

He got a job in a grocery chain store warehouse unloading incoming produce from railroad cars and loading trucks delivering to the retail stores. The pay was at the rate of thrity-two cents an hour while actually engaged in moving produce. You weren't paid for time spent waiting.

During these waiting periods Jimmy and his co-workers mostly grumbled about the hard work and the hard times. Slowly a strategy took shape. Five of the boys, including Jim Hoffa, talked the rest of the warehouse workers into forming a union. The next time a big shipment of highly perishable strawberries arrived at the unloading dock, the new union went out on strike. Jimmy was eighteen.

The following year the Hoffa union was chartered by the Teamsters International as Local 299. As a paid representative of this Local, Hoffa did organizational work and apparently did it well for advances followed and he became President of this Teamster unit in 1937.

In the meantime, he met and married Josephine Poszy-wak and in due course two children, Barbara Ann and James, came along.

After his early successes one promotion led to another and Hoffa moved steadily upward in the Teamsters' Union hierarchy. In 1957 he was elected General President of the International Brotherhood of Teamsters, Chauffeurs, Warehousemen and Helpers of America. Thus he became a very important man indeed.

While compiling this little biography I came upon many references to investigations of Hoffa by the McClellan Committee. Obviously Bobby Kennedy was the key man in these proceedings. I telephoned his office for an appointment but was told to "just drop in and try to catch him." This I did.

A receptionist directed me to Kenneth O'Donnell. A former star football player at Harvard, O'Donnell was then an assistant to Chief Counsel Robert Kennedy. In this instance, he was acting the role of appointment secretary or at least as "screener" of unfamiliar callers.

Kenney O'Donnell did not detain me. We chatted. He asked my business, left me for a minute, returned, and escorted me to Bobby Kennedy.

He was seated behind a desk in the tightly partitioned privacy of a corner of the larger office. There was barely room enough for the second chair, a file cabinet or two, and odd-sized cardboard boxes crammed with papers and stacked unevenly.

I introduced myself by name and he said hello. I don't recall a handshake.

He looked very much as he does now: lots of hair, football nose, and youthful though more fleshy than his photographs. I remember his eyes. They were an unsparkling dusty blue-gray. He looked at me and kept on looking. My memory of his eyes is clear.

Apparently Kenney O'Donnell had briefed him on my mission. He took the initiative by asking for whom I was writing the piece. I told him that it was a ghost job and gave him the name of my agent. His retort was quick and sharp, like a line drive hit back at the pitcher off a slow blooping pitch. "Never heard of him," he cracked. He placed both hands squarely on the edge of the desk in front of him with an air of unequivocal finality.

There is an old anecdote about a man who in a similar situation said: "I never heard of your mother either, but I'm sure she is a very fine woman." I thought better of it and though slightly unnerved went ahead with my list of questions.

His replies were cryptic. He looked bored. He frequently referred me to the printed records of McClellan Committee hearings.

Without consciously planning to do so, I needled Bobby somewhat by asking how he got the job as Chief Counsel of the Committee.

It is worth remembering that this interview took place not long after one of the periodic exposes of nepotism in Washington when the nation is startled anew to learn of the many wives, brothers, sons, daughters, cousins, nephews, nieces, and in-laws on Congressional payrolls. Bobby Kennedy's big brother Senator John F. Kennedy was a prominent member of the McClellan Committee. This is not to say that Bobby might not have found an important job on his own, but merely to relate the facts surrounding his stewardship as Chief Counsel of this Committee and to delineate his character. Both have important bearings on any story about James R. Hoffa.

He said that he had been Chief Counsel of the "full

committee" and had requested and received the same slot on the "Select Committee" when it was formed. I asked how he got the job on the staff of the full committee. He said that he had been Minority Counsel and automatically moved up to Chief Counsel when the Democratic majority took over the Senate in 1954. I asked how he got the job as Minority Counsel. He replied that he had worked for the committee back in early 1953 before leaving to do a stint with the old Hoover Commission which was studying ways and means of streamlining the Federal bureaucracy. I asked him how he got the job on the committee staff back in 1953 and he said "I came over" from the Justice Department.

I wondered how he got the job with the Justice Department being fresh out of the University of Virginia law school and with no experience. Suddenly Bobby was on his feet and the interview was over.

In view of all the harsh things that had been written about Jimmy Hoffa (and who can recall anything favorable?) I did not telephone, but went in person on the theory that it would be harder for them to dismiss me face-to-face than simply hang up on me.

The Teamsters Union building in Washington is a marble and glass palace. It cost a great deal of money to build and it caused a great deal of comment. But the thing that made the greatest impression was its emptiness—not of furniture and fixtures, but of people. Whatever they might say about Jimmy Hoffa, they could never accuse him of featherbedding the home office.

The pretty girl at the front desk had a cryptic telephone conversation with somebody and then turned back to me. "Mr. McCarthy will see you," she said. Mr. McCarthy, she explained, was the public relations director. High heels clicked toward me and I turned as another pretty girl asked me to come with her.

5

Jake McCarthy let me know that Jimmy Hoffa was not exactly enchanted by the request to be interviewed by a writer. "He's suspicious of everybody or anybody in the writing game," Jake said.

On the other hand, I added, when he refuses to be interviewed he runs the risk of being blasted from ambush without even an opportunity to try to soften criticism. "I'm going to write this piece with or without Hoffa's cooperation," was my approach.

Jake questioned me and I told him about my assignment. I said that my plan was to interview Bobby and Jimmy, and to read the transcripts of the McClellan Committee hearings. "Tell you what," he said. "You go ahead and read the transcripts and then come back to me and I'll guarantee that you'll get a good interview with Hoffa."

That seemed fair enough.

At that time there were some forty-five printed volumes of exact question-and-answers transcriptions of the hearings conducted by the "Select Committee on Improper Activities in the Labor and/or Management Field." This special Senate committee was conducting its investigation in order to determine what additional legislation, if any, was needed to govern labor-management relations.

After scanning several of the green-backed volumes and reading some in considerable depth, my attention settled upon Part 36 covering August 5, 6, 7, 8, and 12, 1958. This had to do with an alleged payoff by Detroit laundry owners to somebody high up in the Teamsters Union.

Jimmy Hoffa was the first witness. His initial exchange with committee counsel Robert Kennedy revealed the total lack of rapport between the two men, and the antagonism:

Mr. Kennedy: Mr. Hoffa, did you know Mr. Joseph Holtzman?

Mr. Hoffa: Yes, I did.

Mr. Kennedy: He was a close friend of yours, was he?

Mr. Hoffa: I knew Joe Holtzman.

Mr. Kennedy: He was a close friend of yours?

Mr. Hoffa: I knew Joe Holtzman.

Mr. Kennedy: He was a close friend of yours?

Mr. Hoffa: I knew Joe Holtzman.

Mr. Kennedy: He was a close friend of yours?

Mr. Hoffa: Just a moment. I knew Joe Holtzman, and he wasn't any particular friend of mine.

Mr. Kennedy: Just answer the question.

The hearing transcript revealed something else too; something of far greater importance than the clash of two strong-willed men.

Here are the essential facts in the case under investigation:

1. Detroit laundries, members of a trade association called "The Detroit Institute of Laundry" were negotiating a labor contract with Local 285 of the Teamsters Union. No progress was being made.

2. The Institute's executives (paid employees) advised its' laundry owner members that the dispute could be settled, without a strike, with the payment of $17,500. This money would be given to a professional labor-relations consultant who, presumably, would pass it on to a "higher-up" in the Teamsters Union. It would be a strictly cash transaction.

3. The laundry owners went along with this. The money was collected on a pro-rata basis—so much per truck—and turned over to the Institute's executives. Subsequently, the labor contract was signed.

4. After the money was collected and passed on, but

7

several meetings before the contract was signed, Jimmy Hoffa showed up at one of the negotiating sessions.

Question: Did the money go to Jimmy Hoffa?

Answer: The following is taken from the transcript.

Senator Mundt: Do you know to whom the $90 (per truck) was paid?

Mr. Miller (A laundry owner): Well, I paid it to John Meissner.

Three successive witnesses who had been laundry owners in Detroit at the time and who by their own admission participated in the "payoff" testified that they had paid cash at the rate of $90 per truck. They said that they gave the money to Messers. Meissner and Balkwill, secretary and president of the Detroit Institute of Laundry. One of the owners told the Committee: "I was told it would be given to Mr. Holtzman who was engaged as a labor relations man."

More testimony:

Mr. Kennedy: Did you believe . . . that the payment that you had been making to Mr. Holtzman, at least part of that went to Mr. Hoffa?

Mr. Balkwill: Well, we wouldn't have any right to say that it did.

Mr. Kennedy: Where did you believe the money was going?

Mr. Balkwill: Well, we knew it went to Mr. Holtzman.

* * * *

Mr. Kennedy: You believed that it was to go to Mr. Hoffa?

Mr. Balkwill: Well, I wouldn't make that statement either.

* * * *

Everybody agreed that labor relations consultant Joseph Holtzman had received $17,500 in cold cash. Nobody knew what he did with it. Nobody on the Senate side of the table would assume that he had earned it honestly in his capacity as a labor relations consultant and could do as he pleased with it. Nobody on the witness side of the table would say that all or any part of it found its way to Jimmy Hoffa.

A torturous day-and-a-half of ardent and often leading questioning led literally to a dead end. Joseph Holtzman, alas, was in his grave. One of the good Senators serving on the committee exclaimed in exasperation: "I am looking for a live witness who knows something about this." Bobby Kennedy did not produce such a witness.

. . . and one final commentary on who got the money:

Mr. Kennedy: There is a situation in this case where, according to the testimony, no hearsay whatsoever but the sworn testimony of yesterday, there was a payment made of $17,500, a payoff, in order to get an intervention from a higher-up in the Teamsters Union. Then you intervened. Can you give us—

Mr. Hoffa: What does that mean?

Mr. Kennedy: Can you give us any more explanation of that?

Mr. Hoffa: What does that mean? That I got the $17,-500? Is that what you are insinuating? If you do, I did not get it.

Mr. Kennedy: You did not get that money?

Mr. Hoffa: And I deny under oath that I got it.

Mr. Kennedy: You did not get any of the money?

Mr. Hoffa: I did not.

Meanwhile, America's newspaper readers were seeing headlines such as the one appearing on the front page of the Washington (D. C.) Post, August 6, 1958:

which simply was not a correct interpretation of the results of the proceedings. It would have been more accurate to report: "Witnesses *Fail* To Link Hoffa To Payoff."

At this point I knew that I couldn't go through with the assignment. I could not, on the basis of what I then knew, sit down at my typewriter and knock out an anti-Hoffa screed—not even a ghost job.

Nevertheless, I claimed my interview with Jimmy Hoffa. His office was L-shaped, big and uncluttered. The short leg of the L was furnished with a big, rectangular desk. An executive type chair was behind it and four arm chairs lined parallel in front of it. The long leg of the L was furnished with two sofas and some easy chairs arranged in a conversation group around a low table.

Along the wall on the tall side of the L stood a row of polished wooden cabinets slightly more than waist-high. On top of a cabinet and leaning against the wall rested a framed printing of a famed quotation:

"If I were to try to read, much less answer, all the attacks made on me, this shop might as well be closed for any other business. I do the very best I know how —the very best I can; and I mean to keep doing so until the end. If the end brings me out all right, what is said against me won't amount to anything. If the end brings me out wrong, ten angels swearing I was right would make no difference."

As I read the printed by-line, "A. Lincoln," Jimmy Hoffa bounded (no other word describes a Hoffa entrance) into the room peeling off his suit coat.

His physical appearance was powerful. He was broad and muscular. His head was set solidly on wide shoulders.

His hair was black and bristley. His eyes were gray-blue and bright. His forearms were heavily muscled all the way to the wrists and appeared abnormally long in a short sleeved shirt. His right hand was badly scared.

Jake introduced us and I got a knuckle-shattering hand shake, a wide toothy smile, and a surprisingly high-pitched how-do-you-do. He sat down in the big chair behind the desk while Jake began explaining that I was going to write a piece about him.

He didn't looked pleased and he didn't look unhappy either. He looked like a man who had taken a helluva lot and could take plenty more, right now if necessary. His expression was neutral, bland, and at the same time challenging. As Jake talked Hoffa nodded his head continuously and murmured, "fine, fine; all right, all right; okay, okay."

When Jake stopped talking Hoffa just looked at me and waited. My move.

I began by asking if the pressure of the Senate hearings was getting him down. I remember his reply because it sounded more cocky than true. "It don't bother me one bit," he said emphatically, adding for good measure; "Not a bit." He gestured with a slight sweeping movement of his right hand.

I told him that I had been reading the transcripts of the testimony about the laundry payoff in Detroit. "Who do you think got the money?" I asked.

Hoffa said that he'd be damned if he knew. Then he added that he had heard the testimony and read it too. So far as he could see, he said, the laundry owners gave the money to their own hired executives who testified that they had paid it to Joseph Holtzman for "services rendered." He seemed impatient: "What the hell. I get paid for being General President of this International; Bobby Kennedy takes a salary from the taxpayers; you're not here for your health; so why shouldn't Holtzman get paid for his work?"

11

The funny part of the deal, and the thing that made it smell, I said, was the cash transaction. "What's so funny about cash?" Hoffa demanded. He remarked that he liked cash and it occurred to me that if some of the things his critics said were true, this might be the understatement of the generation. Maybe he sensed my thinking for his next comment was: "Nobody has to worry about my finances—the Internal Revenue boys take care of that."

There was no need and nothing to be gained by trying to cover the same ground that was plowed by the McClellan Committee. The most to be gained from this interview was exposure to an unique and powerful personality. I stayed as long as I could drag out the interview, asking any question that came into my head.

He rose to the bait and began rambling about the thing he knows best—the Teamsters' Union.

Jimmy Hoffa is a businessman. The Teamsters Union is big business and he is chairman of the board and chief executive officer. He bragged to me that his "boys" had gained more than any other union's members in wages, fringe benefits, and generally favorable working conditions. He showed me charts to prove his points. He talked about Teamster membership figures. "The rest of them are losing and we're gaining," he told me. In the union business the payoff is membership. Gain members and you ride high; lose members and you're in trouble with your board.

Jimmy Hoffa laughed when I made reference to charges of dictatorship in the world of the Teamster Union. "Ludicrous," he exclaimed, and repeated the word which he apparently liked. "Hell," he expanded, "I called Sandy O'Brien in Chicago and told him that I wanted them to cooperate with us to get this political action program off the ground. He told me to go to hell—said they'd have their own political action program. What kind of dictatorship is that?" He gave assurance, as strong men are wont to do, that he couldn't even dictate to his wife.

He worked at maintaining a calm exterior but as he talked his face was a picture window to storms inside. His eyes could be hard or soft. His smile; warm sometimes and sometimes chilly. He gestured with head and hands. Often his chin moved up and down in a gentle or vigorous nod and his hands swept the air before him like windshield wipers as he emphasized his statements.

The Jimmy Hoffa personality did not capture me. It intrigued me and it puzzled me. Here was a strong man, manager of a huge and potent organization, whose name appeared daily in the news in a derogatory context. True or false, what must it do to a man's mind and heart to know that his wife, children and friends see this and hear it at every turn? This question fixed itself in my brain and around it whirled another: Who is the real Jimmy Hoffa?

Who is the real Jimmy Hoffa?

CHAPTER 2

Generations
of
Hoffas

You might say he delivered himself. He arrived under his own power, struggling and squalling. A friend of his mother who sometimes served the neighborhood as a midwife or "practical nurse" was on hand. The doctor came at the very last minute. He had said in the beginning, and until undisputably refuted by violent pre-natal kicking, that the swelling in her abdomen was a tumor. Her first words, she remembers, after the pain and shock and exhaustion had subsided, were, "some tumor."

It was early on a cold morning at Brazil, Indiana on February 14, 1913. Jimmy was a full nine-month baby, according to his mother, weighing seven pounds and six ounces.

He was the third of four children born to John and Viola Hoffa. Jennetta was three. Billy was eighteen months. And Nancy was to follow a year later.

He was named after his Uncle Jim on his father's side and Riddle, his mother's family name. James Riddle Hoffa.

Jimmy's father, John Cleveland Hoffa, was of the third generation of Hoffas who made their homes in the harsh countryside of southwest Indiana. Earlier generations had lived in Pennsylvania, where, family tradition has it, they were among the Pennsylvania Dutch settlers.

14

Jimmy's great grandparents, John and Mary Cook Hoffa, were caught up in the brush fire westward movement of the new nation. About 1835 they boarded a flat-bottom boat at Pittsburgh and drifted with the current of the Ohio River toward new opportunity and a new life. They were pioneers in Owen County, Indiana.

John and Mary made their first home in Indiana in a mud-chinked log cabin of one room and a half-loft on rented farm land in the northern part of the county near the cross-roads village of Cunot. As their fortunes improved they moved to better and better dwellings, always in the Cunot neighborhood.

This was and remains hard and hilly country, unkind to farmers. But, as the Hoffas were not farmers, the quality of the soil was of little concern to them from the standpoint of family fortunes. John Hoffa found employment in keeping with his skill and taste as a blacksmith. In five generations of Hoffas in the direct line of decendancy of James Riddle Hoffa, they have seriously engaged in farming only as a last resort in severely hard times or as gentlemen farmers when they were prosperous.

John Hoffa was not an under-the-spreading-chestnut-tree type of blacksmith. He did not have a shop in the village and children did not stand by in awe, watching the sparks fly and singing to the music of his hammer and anvil. He was a mine blacksmith, meaning that he specialized in serving the metal work needs of coal mines. This included shoeing the cantankerous mine mules but more particularly, sharpening picks, repairing other hand tools, maintaining the simple machinery used at the time, and manufacturing on-the-spot metal devices such as hinges, pins, hooks, chain links, etc. He followed his work by muleback, making the rounds from one mine pit to another in Owen, Clay and Putnam counties.

Jimmy's great grandfather may or may not have been the first Hoffa to settle in southwest Indiana. Certainly he was among the first for permanent residents were extremely scarce before well into the 1800's. But others of the same family came too. By mid-century a generous scattering of Hoffas populated both Owen and Clay counties. It is assumed by members of the family that all of them were related.

Court House records of the two counties abound with references to the affairs of the Hoffas. The crisp, crumbling, yellow documents of the public and legal business of citizens of Owen County are complete and continuous since 1819. Clay County records were destroyed by fire in 1851, but those filed from that date to this are there for all to see, beginning in the hand drawn flourishes of quill pen and pokeberry ink and continuing today in the precise, impersonal type of modern machines.

Around the 1850's the Hoffas emerged as artisans, businessmen, traders and prominent citizens of the two counties.

One Jacob Hoffa (not in Jimmy's direct line) died in the year 1859 leaving a sizable estate to be divided among six sons and two daughters who were charged with keeping his widow in comfort and plenty. During his eighty-odd years Jacob had accumulated land, livestock, personal property, and a mercantile business. It is noteworthy that he did not own slaves although he was a well-to-do man and most certainly could have if he had wanted to.

The given names of Jacob's offspring are of interest for they indicate how far the family had come from their German homeland. Clearly it had been in America long enough for the melting pot to do its work. Instead of Hermann, Ludwig, Helmut, Anna and Huldah, the children were tagged with Jacob, Aaron, John, Jeremiah, Issac, Abraham, Catherine and Sarah.

The Deed Books and Civil Case Indexes of Clay and

Owen County records list many business transactions of Hoffas. John and Issac, especially, were wheeler-dealers in Clay County. Records of their businesses, notes, collections, mortgages and foreclosures dot the musty pages.

Other Hoffas bought and sold land, usually at a profit, and secured licenses to operate businesses.

The Criminal Index of Owen County does not mention the name Hoffa. If any member of the family committed a crime there from 1819 to 1965, he got away with it. But Clay County Hoffas were not so pure or so fortunate. On October 6, 1927 at Brazil, Indiana, Clyde Hoffa was hauled into court on a criminal count. He was found guilty of passing a school bus.

The Hoffas of Clay County sent two sons to war on the Union side in the War Between the States. Samuel and John enlisted in "I" Company of the 133rd Indiana Regiment. This was a unit of "100 day volunteers," mustered May 17, 1864. They mustered out at the end of their enlistment and apparently thus ended Samuel's military career. But John joined up with "B" Company of the 149th Indiana, where he was commissioned a Second Lieutenent and promoted through the ranks to Captain and Company Commander.

Captain Hoffa's company served on occupation duty at Decatur, Alabama and was mustered out on September 18, 1865 at Nashville, Tennessee.

Jimmy's grandfather was Jacob Henry Hoffa. He was born January 25, 1848 in a gaunt, unpainted frame house on rented farm land near Cunot. He grew up there doing the things that country boys did then and do now. He ran in the woods, swam in the creek, jumped in the hay, slid on the ice, and climbed anything that stood upright and taller than himself, especially young saplings ripe to be ridden to the ground. He chased rabbits in summer and tracked them in the snow in winter. He kept an old hound dog who helped him tree possums and coons and caught them when he shook them down. They were penned and "cleaned" for a week or more by feeding before their inevitable fate—the frying skillet or the boiling pot.

Jake loved the outdoors and he bequeathed this deep affection through his son to the present generation of Hoffas.

Jake did the chores that were demanded of him by his mother, Mary Cook Hoffa, a stern frontier woman. Perhaps these were more than for most boys, even farm boys in mid-century of the 1800's, since his father, a mine blacksmith, was away from home for days sometimes and sometimes weeks. These duties loomed large in his memory when he was an old, old man.

The household water had to be toted from a spring. This was his first responsibility. It was years before there was a well with a pump. The wood box had to be kept full and this, too, was Jake's job from the time he was strong enough to carry it. Wood chopping came only slightly later when he could handle the six-pound axe with relative safety and efficiency.

He plowed, planted and weeded a vegetable garden, and gathered its bounty in due time. He was a hunter, for the family depended on wood and field for meat for the table. Rabbits, squirrels, coons, and possums were the mainstay. Occasionally young Jake was lucky enough to bag one of the pigs that ran near-wild in the woods. He was an excellent shot with the huge muzzle loader but the razorbacks were as wily as they were ferocious.

Somehow he managed to attend school long enough and with sufficient diligence to learn to read and write quite fluently; a commendable achievement at the time and place, for a boy of such circumstances.

Somehow, too, he met, courted and married Nancy

Jane Asher, the daughter of a well known and prosperous farmer in the Cunot community. The Ashers, also, were among the early settlers of Owen County. Their lineage traces easily back through Kentucky, Blount County in East Tennessee, and into North Carolina.

When the Ashers came to Indiana they brought property and wealth; a very unusual thing for immigrants in any time or in any land. Well-to-do people stay where they have wealth and stature. It's the poor people who blaze trails to new frontiers.

Jake Hoffa was barely weaned when he began accompanying his father on work trips of short duration to nearby mines. Smithy tools and materials were not unfamiliar to him. They had been his first playthings and smithy talk had dominated household conversation since before his earliest memory.

He was strong and eager. He pumped the bellows, fetched and carried, and made himself generally useful to his father. When, at last, he was old enough to decide upon his own life's work there was never any question as to what it would be.

He served an informal apprenticeship to his father and the smithy trade came easily. He hired out as a full-fledged blacksmith before his twentieth birthday.

Jacob Henry Hoffa kept his trade and it kept him throughout his life span of seventy-three years, six months and nineteen days. He passed away of natural causes on August 19, 1921 at Brazil, Indiana. His remains were returned to Cunot for burial in the land of his father and his youth.

He was survived by two sons and numerous grandchildren. He had outlived his youngest, John Cleveland Hoffa, by nearly a year.

* * *

When Johnny was born the Jacob Hoffa family was

19

living near Cunot. Their house had four large rooms and an outside "summer" kitchen. There was a small barn, a pig sty and pen, chicken coops and pens, and other nondescript outbuildings.

The inside walls of the house were rough plastered, unpainted, and generally unadorned. The outside of pine slab was painted white or whitewashed at irregular intervals. The auxiliary buildings were weathered to a silver grey. There was a picket fence out front.

Large hardwood trees stood close to shade the house and yard from summer's sun. A good sized peach tree near the barn bore fruit of such quality as to be much looked forward to by the entire family. An iron rim from a wagon wheel hung from a length of rope tied to a stout limb of the big tree closest to the back door. The ground beneath was packed clean and smooth in line with the arc of the "swing."

There was a large vegetable garden and one field was kept free of scrub growth for pasture and wild hay. (The Hoffas kept a cow and a mule.)

The Hoffas were not inclined toward having scrawny children and Jacob's were not an exception to the rule. James, Charles, and John were big for their ages and strong. They grew up in a time when boys of ten or thereabouts, depending on their size, were called upon to do the work of men. This was doubly true in their case because their father was away from home so much of the time.

On weekends or whenever he happened to be at home for a day or two, Jacob looked over the place and gave detailed instructions for work to be done in his absence. When he was packed and ready to go again, when the mule was hitched and the wagon stood at the gate, he always had this parting admonition: "Boys, take care of the place and mind your mother."

There was wood to be chopped and carried, water to be pumped, livestock to be fed and bedded, a cow to be milked twice every day, and the vegetable garden to be tended. The Hoffa boys did their work. Punishment for not-doing or wrong-doing was swift, sure and severe. But this was the way of life for virtually all country boys in those times.

Boyhood was brief and hard in the 1880's and '90's.

Nancy Asher Hoffa to her everlasting credit insisted that her sons take advantage of educational opportunities available to them. Nevertheless, education was primarily a wintertime activity for her children as well as others in the community. Spring planting of necessity took precedence over everything, resulting in much absenteeism from mid-April until summer vacation began. Classes resumed in September, but that was the beginning of the harvest season and so it was nearly November before the teacher held one last review and went on to new work.

The Hoffa boys attended a wood frame school building within a mile and a quarter of their home. This was considered well within "walking distance" and that is how they came and went to school and home. Six grades were taught by a single teacher in one room. All three of the Hoffa boys completed these six grades and went on to "high" school in Cloverdale. There they were graduated from the ninth grade.

* * *

Ben Merchon was a coal prospector. His headquarters was Brazil but his operating territory covered several counties in the southwest Indiana coal fields. Ben's steam-powered drilling rig required the skill and strength of two good, reliable men. John Cleveland Hoffa was the second man in the Ben Merchon drilling business. He and Ben travelled together in their work.

Late in the summer of 1908 their prospecting took them to Parke County in the vicinity of Jessup. They took room and board in the West home. The Riddle farm was down the road a short distance.

Elizabeth West and Voila Riddle were best girl friends although Lizzie was two years younger than "Ola." At eighteen Viola was practically an old maid, which may account for her friend's eagerness to introduce her to an eligible man. Lizzie couldn't wait to tell "Ola": "There's a nice young man staying at our house!"

He was a handsome man. Dark, very dark eyes set level below a high forehead and thick, black hair combed back and parted on the left side, were his most striking features at first glance.

He was six feet tall and weighed about one hundred and ninety pounds. His shoulders were broad and thick and sloped in the manner characteristic of powerfully muscular men. But for all his mass and muscle his pictures show a lithe, graceful man and he is so remembered.

John Hoffa was a good deal more handsome than is his son Jimmy. Jimmy looks more like his mother, who was a pretty girl and is a handsome woman, but the features that flatter a woman often aren't so becoming on a man.

The Riddle and the West families were close personally as well as geographically. Viola and Lizzie visited back and forth nearly every day and often several times a day. There was always an errand to be done or something to be told. Now Viola found more things than usual to take her there, especially in the early evening after supper, when the men were home from work and at their leisure.

She was a quiet and bashful girl but she was also a young woman ready for marriage. Instinct overcame shyness and produced the necessary will power to guide her hesitant footsteps within noticing range of Lizzie's lodger.

And he noticed. John looked up from his reading, turned away from his man talk, or paused over his whittling. She did not have to make a second trip to catch his eye.

He called on Viola almost every evening during the remainder of his stay at the West home. Soon it was known that John Hoffa, the coal drilling man, was courting the Riddle girl.

John was nearly twenty-eight years old. Up to now he had shown no inclination toward marriage and had not expressed a desire to enter the holy estate. But now he had found a prize, and he knew it.

There was never a hint of opposition from Viola's parents, or anyone else, for that matter. She was of marrying age, he was an eligible man, and the Hoffas were a fine, old family, well known throughout the area. Steve and Jennetta Riddle accepted their future son-in-law at face value—an honest, healthy, working man—and welcomed him into their home.

George H. James, President of the Times Publishing Company and Editor Emeritus of the *Brazil Daily Times,* came to Clay County in 1910. "There *were* plenty of Hoffas," he recalls, adding with a change of tense which instantaneously reviews half a century, "and they *are* law abiding, good people around here."

Such was the good name of his family when John Hoffa courted Viola Riddle.

The Ben Merchon drilling company had a lot of work in Parke County during the rest of that year. John saw her almost every weekend and sometimes on week days too. Viola doesn't remember his proposal. It seems that he was serious right from the start and their marriage came naturally as if in a sequence of predestined events, on May 15, 1909.

Their first home was the old pine slab house with the picket fence out front and the peach tree out back near the barn. With four large rooms it was plenty big for Jacob and Nancy and for John and their new daughter-in-law, too. The old folks were glad to have them.

John's way of life was little changed. He still worked for Ben Merchon and was away from home and Viola much of the time. Viola quickly made a place for herself in the Hoffa household. She said little, listened much, and did more than her share of the work. An unspoken, undemonstrative, unsophisticated affection developed between Viola and her parents-in-law which was no less genuine for these guileless qualities.

They lived in the house of his parents for about a year. Jennetta was born there. Soon after this blessed event they moved to the old Asher place about two miles away.

During this period a major family decision was taking shape. After three quarters of a century the family was shaking itself loose from the Cunot community.

Jacob, the patriarch, led the way. The mobile life of a mine blacksmith had grown tiring in his autumnal years. When an opportunity came for him to take over a stationary blacksmith shop on Main Street in Brazil, he jumped at it.

Within a few months four new Hoffa households were established in Brazil. (Other Hoffas were there already but they were distant cousins, unclaimed and unclaiming.) Jake and Nancy, John and Viola, James and Ella, and Charles and Ruth found houses within an area of two blocks.

Brazil, like all towns large or small, had distinct geographic divisions bearing names of convenience or mockery. There was the usual Downtown; the business district. There were suburban communities, Donaldsville, Knightsville, and Harmony, barely reached by main thorough-fares stretching out like fingers from a palm to touch them. And there was The Hill, as the well-to-do and the social climbers liked to call their part of town. (They were aware that it was called Bankrupt Hill, too, but they considered that the voice of jealousy and were more flattered than hurt by it.)

The Hoffas found houses to rent in a northeast section inhabited by miners and other semi-skilled and laboring people. The streets meandered north from East Main Street, conveniently contouring to the landscape like fallen kite strings. The Hoffas lived in Stringtown.

John and Viola lived on North Vandalia Street in a three room, A-frame house. Doors were centered from front to back through the living room, bedroom, and kitchen. Open all the doors and you could shoot a shotgun right down the middle through the whole house without hitting anything.

Jimmy Hoffa was born in the middle room of this particular Shotgun house in Stringtown in Brazil, Indiana.

CHAPTER *3*

Young
Jimmy
Hoffa

The first seven years of Jimmy Hoffa's life were his father's last years. They were good years for the family. Until the final months, they were prosperous and happy years. Jimmy was walking at nine months and jabbering with Billy and Jennetta, aged two and three respectively. At twelve months he was talking in the language that mothers understand.

The children were almost too close together to be called stairsteps. The step down from Jennetta to Billy to Jimmy to Nancy was so slightly graduated that they were more like four close following ripples on a millpond.

Jimmy and his brother and sisters remember bits and pieces making up a pleasant portrait of their father. He was away most of the time. But when he was at home for a few days or a weekend it was like a holiday. He walked and talked with them and played their games. He took them fishing on Fish Creek near Harmony. He took them to Grandpa Hoffa's blacksmith shop on Main Street. If a circus or a medicine show was in town they were sure to see it. He made things for them of wood and leather with his two-blade Barlow knife.

The family changed houses twice during this seven-year period. They gave up the little "shotgun" house on Vandalia in favor of an only slightly more elegant place one block east on Ashley Street. The house stands today, a monument to ugliness and neglect. It is better to think of it as it was fifty years ago.

It was a T-shaped building with two rooms across the front and another centered in back. The front elevation gave it the appearance of a larger house than it actually was: it was a high-built house. An unusually tall window was centered on each side of the front door and the roof was high pitched. The house was painted barn red. The wooden shingled roof was weathered grey.

The enclosed back porch featured a built-in water pump, hand operated, of course. There were two out-buildings. One was a shed for coal and wood and general storage. The other was *the* outhouse.

Inside, the walls were thickly plastered and papered. The floor was double thick and tight. The windows were tight. It was a well-built, snug house.

Their second move could not have been made except as a result of improved family fortunes. It was to a much larger house on Church Street beyond the unofficial borders of Stringtown.

It was square and white painted with four spacious rooms and enclosed porches front and back. The roof was low pitched, wood shingled. The inside walls were solidly plastered and brightly papered. The floors were pretty and smooth.

The yard was small, but large enough for clothes lines and work space. Play area was no problem for all the neighborhood children played all over the neighborhood.

This house was conveninetly located only half a block from the Lambert Street School.

Jennetta, Billy and Jimmy began their formal educa-

27

tion in Brazil. Nancy did too, attending a private kindergarten rather than the public school.

Miss Ada Brough was the Supervisor of grades one through three in the Brazil school system. Her methods included classroom visitations on a continuing, rotating schdule to some fifteen rooms. She remembers the Hoffa children.

One day in a first grade classroom at Lambert Street, Miss Ada supervised a lesson in writing. It was early in the school year and the children were just learning to write their names. Miss Ada grasped a chubby little hand in hers and spelled out the letters, J-A-M-E-S H-O-F-F-A.

Jimmy made a lasting impression on Miss Ada Brough. After that day she went out of her way to notice him and to keep up with his progress. These are her memories of Jimmy Hoffa at ages six and seven:

"He was a lovely looking boy. Just a cherub."
"I visited fifteen rooms and he was the best."
"He was a quiet, attentive child."
"It's funny, I can remember his handwriting."
"Always neat and clean—more so than average."
"He wrote so beautifully."
"It is so definite that he was best."

* * * *

Terrible sickness and death came to the family in 1920 when Jimmy's father was struck down suddenly, unexpectedly.

John had gone on a work trip with Ben Merchon. When he said goodby he had been as hearty and happy as always. A week later Viola looked out through the kitchen window, and much to her surprise saw him entering the yard. He was unsteady on his feet, like a drunk man. But he did not drink—it was a comparison, not an accusation, that went through Viola's mind.

He had a strange look, a kind of broken look, that startled her. She turned away and then back again to get another, a fresh impression. At second glance she knew instantly that whatever it was that ailed John, it was a serious thing. She ran to meet him. When they entered the house she led him directly to his bed.

Local physicians were at a loss to diagnose an ailment that was not accompanied by chills or fever, without cuts, bruises or broken bones. After some discussion among members of the family, John was taken to a hospital.

Hindsight, of course, has twenty-twenty vision. Looking back through four decades and four years of advances in the medical profession, it is probable that John's semi-dazed condition and his broken physical condition resulted from a moderately massive stroke. It is probable that it was never diagnosed. And it is probable that the hospital was little more than an uncomforting place of confinement.

Viola went to see him twice at the hospital. It was a day-long journey by train or trolley, and it wasn't easy for her to get away from work (she had begun taking in laundry) and the children.

Viola could not at that time remember a single person who went to a hospital as a patient and came back alive. It is doubtful that she knew anyone, directly or indirectly, who had. To the country people of southwest Indiana, hospitals were places of last resort. She had opposed John's admission but had given in to the persuasion of other members of the family. Now, when she visited there, she found the hospital a mysterious and forbidding place. When told that she could not see her husband she protested, but was turned back by the unyielding authority of hospital personnel.

But the second time she made up her mind that she was going to see him and that nobody was going to stop her. The attendant told her that she could not see him.

She did not argue and perhaps the attendant thought she was leaving. However, she had noticed a little office occupied by an official-looking, important-looking person, and she went right in and up to him. It happened to be John's attending physician.

He advised her not to insist on seeing John. "He won't recognize you anyway," he said.

"Whether he knows me or not," Viola said, "I will know him."

They walked up a flight of stairs and down a long, long darkened room between rows of beds. A patient was lying or lounging on each bed. At last they approached and halted before a bed whose occupant lay with his back to them.

"Johnny, I think you've got a visitor," the doctor said.

"I'm glad of it," he responded, turning to see.

Viola moved closer in a fearsome moment of wondering if he would know her.

"Where have you been?" he asked.

"I've been so far away, Johnny, I couldn't get here."

"Where am I?"

"You're in a hospital."

"Why did you let them take me here, Buddy?"

"Well, Johnny, at the time we thought it was best you should go."

"Come here, Buddy. I want to talk to you."

Viola looked at the doctor who nodded and gestured with his eyes while moving to a discreet distance. She drew a chair close to the bed and leaned her face close to his. There was more sadness than pain in his deep, dark eyes.

"You know and I know that I am not going to live much longer," he began. So carefully thought, so clearly spoken, each word stood stark and alone as though waiting for the following word to catch up.

"Johnny, we brought you here to get well," Viola tried vainly to cheer him.

"Well, I know I'm not and you do too."

During a long pause he drew in deep breaths.

"Now, I want you to promise me two things," he continued.

"What are they, Johnny?"

"I don't want to be taken to the undertakers first," he said. "When I'm brought home, bring me home first."

As Viola nodded her promise, he added: "I want to be put away in all black."

No clock could tick as slowly as the moments passed in the long pause before his next words.

"Buddy, provide a home and keep the children."

"I will, Johnny, you know I'll do that."

"One more thing—and—you promise me anyway you want to."

Pause.

"What is it, Johnny?"

"Carry my name to the grave."

"Johnny—I don't know—I am still young, and I don't know what the future will do to me—but if I keep my mind as I have it now, I will."

They didn't talk much more.

*   *   *   *

Several days later Viola had the awful premonition. She had felt it coming on during the uneasy, fretful night. Now, as she was hanging wet wash on the clothesline, she felt it very strongly.

Something unknown and compelling caused her to pause in her work and to look past the house and down the street. A telegraph delivery boy was coming. Her heart lumped in her throat as he drew nearer, looking at every house number as he came. He went on by, then turned, and came back to their house. She signed for the telegram and in an instant her premonition was verified. Her husband had passed away.

She was glad that the children were spending the day at their Uncle Jim's farm. Jim was in town doing errands and she got word to him at once. He said that he would take care of things and went to make arrangements with the undertaker.

A short time later Jim and Mr. Miller, the undertaker, came to talk with Viola. They said that it would be four the next morning before John's body could be brought home. "I don't care what time the train gets in in the morning," Viola declared, "I want to have him at home before he goes to the undertaker's."

Mr. Miller advised her that it might be much more convenient and satisfactory to take him directly from the train to the parlor, but she was adamant. He had to come home first.

The body was brought directly from the depot to the house on Church Street where Viola was alone with him for the last time. She had been advised, even admonished, by Jim and Mr. Miller not to look at the body, but now she broke her promise.

32

She saw a man with hardly any skin on him. He was close to bones and his back was covered with bedsores. She was filled with remorse for having consented to his admission to the hospital.

The close-knit clan of Jacob Hoffa and many of their far-flung cousins gathered in Brazil for the funeral. Viola's family and friends came too. All together some fifteen motor cars and as many buggies followed the horse-drawn hearse as it turned onto East Main Street, drove slowly past the Court House, past the newspaper office, past Jake's blacksmith shop and the hardware store, past the livery stable, and on out West Main to the cemetery.

Late in the afternoon, after the last of the family and friends had murmured their sympathy and departed, Viola called her children to her. They stood in a little half-circle in front of her chair. She came right to the point and in the simple, direct language they were used to hearing from her, she told them that henceforth she would be both mother and father to them. "You'll all have to help," she said. The matter was discussed no further then or later.

There were many pressing problems. The rent was due, there were bills accumulated during the last four months, cash was needed for groceries, and every day brought new and unexpected demands—the preemptive demands of four small children attending school. There was no time for a formal period of mourning. She concealed her grief so completely that only her closest friends were aware that she suffered excruciating sorrow and remorse. Lizzie Guinn *nee* West tried for months to snap her out of it but she would not be consoled. Work was her only solace; the children's well being was her only pleasure.

The problem of just keeping the family together was immediate and great. There was no money and nobody in or outside of the family had any to offer. Although no one who knows Viola Hoffa can imagine her accepting charity she was not in the least tempted to do so because none was offered. There was no welfare, no relief, no work projects, no surplus food distribution, no nothing except her own strength and ingenuity. The only way to lighten the load would have been for her to apply for her children's admission to an orphanage. But this possibility never crossed her mind.

Their home on Church Street had housed the family during its happiest years. It was the biggest and the prettiest home they had ever had, and also the most expensive. Now, in the interest of economy, Viola did not hesitate to give it up. They moved promptly to the flat over Grandpa Hoffa's blacksmith shop. Soon afterwards they moved back to the old "shotgun" house on Vandalia Street—their first home in Brazil and now their last.

For Jimmy and the other children life went on pretty much as before. Perhaps in their daily routines there was an intensity that wasn't there before; a stepping up of tempo in chores. Maybe there was a change of diet, with more beans and potatoes and less meat and cake. Perhaps shoe soles wore thinner and sweaters more threadbare. But such adjustments, however difficult for adults and hurtful for parents, are taken in stride by children. Certainly among the Hoffa children there was no sense of deprivation. Jimmie especially, was a happy, cheerful boy.

Viola arose first in the morning. How she always awakened just when she wanted to was one of the mysteries of Jimmy Hoffa's young life. Jennetta was next up followed by Jimmy and Billy, and finally Nancy. They made their sleepy way into the kitchen, dressing en route.

A huge, black Garland cooking range dominated the kitchen. It greatly influenced the daily affairs of the entire family. Jimmy and Billy split kindling for it and hauled in both wood and coal, and hauled out ashes. This was a never ending chore. The girls helped with the cooking and their regular job was keeping it clean, which is to say, black. At least once a week they blackened the body of the stove and the pipes and polished the nickle trim.

The stove had a reservoir on one side which supplied hot water for their Saturday bath. Four to a half dozen of Viola's flat irons sat upright in back, always warming and ready for her ironing. The warming ovens high up in back kept homemade bread, cake and pies just right for the big Sunday dinner.

Breakfast was usually fried or scrambled eggs, thick slices of bread toasted on top of the stove, and milk. Around hog-killing time there might be sausage from Uncle Jim's or Grandpa Riddle's farm and now and then heavy slices of crisp Indiana bacon. There's none as good anywhere.

Corn meal mush was a family favorite. It might be served along with the eggs or separately with butter and syrup but any way it was dished up, all the children loved it.

Jimmy had the appetite of a mine mule at sundown except that he was that way all day long. He ate often and much of anything available. In addition to his home consumption, which was substantial since in addition to three meals a day the children were free to raid the ice box, he had an uncanny knack of acquiring food outside of the household. It went without saying that apples, pears, and other domestic fruit that hung over fences, over sidewalks, alleys and other public domain was fair game for any boy under sixteen and Jimmy was barely eight. Also, every wild fruit tree within two miles of Stringtown was on his itinerary in its season. Wild cherries, plums, knotty pears, crab apples, hickory nuts, black walnuts and wild strawberries were important items in his diet.

He and Billy were expert hunters and fishermen by birthright and blood. Even at eight and nine Jimmy could and did snare rabbits and birds with such alacrity that they were regular items on the family menu. The fishing around Brazil wasn't anything to brag about but later, after they moved to Clinton, the Wabash River was the source of many a meal for the entire family.

Jimmy had other talents as a provider. On one memorable occasion he begged a quarter from his mother—no mean feat under the best of circumstances and an impossible one except with perfect timing. In this instance Jimmy took advantage of Lizzie Guinn's presence and with her support ("You can't take it with you," Lizzie said to Viola) his mother gave in.

They were at a Sunday School picnic and Jimmy wanted the quarter to buy a raffle ticket. Clutching the coin he charged through the crowd to where the Deacon held the jar of raffle tickets and the money. Handing over his quarter he jammed his chubby forearm deep into the jar. His fingers, directed by boyish instinct and confidence, sought out a particular wad of folded paper. At the drawing half an hour later guess who won the five-dollar basket of groceries? Five dollars worth in 1923 was about as much as a little boy could carry.

The family liked to visit Uncle Jim or Grandpa Riddle, both of whom had farms near Brazil. Viola and her brood would take the trolley all the way out Main Street to the beginning of Harmony Road, there to be met by Grandpa Riddle with his one-horse wagon, or a horse-drawn sleigh when snow was on the ground.

When the weather was nice Jimmy and Billy sometimes made the trip alone, walking all the way from the end of the trolley line, down a long, straight, cedar lined road known to them as Shady Lane, about a mile to Grandpa Riddle's place or a half to three-quarters of a mile farther to Uncle Jim's.

Jimmy was born with the Hoffa's love of the outdoors.

Those days in the country are his most sentimental memories of childhood. Even as a very small boy of seven, eight and nine, he felt secure and at home in the dark woods. He seemed to have a built-in compass to find his way to and from the many secret places and when the big bell rang out to call men from the fields or children from their play he sped to the house in a straight line from wherever he was.

Jimmy bears a permanent scar on his right hand attesting to one of his visits to his Uncle Jim's farm. It was Sunday morning and the family had gathered for a big Sunday dinner. Chickens had to be killed and cleaned and Jimmy and Billy were proud to be allowed to help. They caught a fat pullet and Jimmy held her by the head and feet, stretching her neck across the chopping block. The axe was pretty heavy for Billy. He got it up all right, but it came down in more of a fall than a swing. The end of the handle behind his hands caught in a hole at the knee of his overalls, the arc wavered, and Jimmy's right hand was laid open.

It was a very bad cut, slicing through bones and tendons on the back of his hand close to the knuckles. It bled profusely. His mother took one look and called to Uncle Jim to get the Model T cranked up. She bandaged it with clean strips from an old bed sheet but the blood soaked through faster than she could wrap it. She compressed it as tightly as she could, trying to control the bleeding, while they rushed to the doctor.

The doctor stopped the bleeding, pressed the wound together, and took a few stitches. He frankly doubted that Jimmy would ever regain full use of the hand. Obviously, he didn't know his patient. Oh, it hurt when he tried to use it and it ached when the weather was a certain way and at night when he let himself think about it. But, gradually after many months of semi-crippleness, normal use of the hand returned and Jimmy forgot about it. Only the giant scar remains. Its tissue pads the knuckles of his right hand.

Jimmy and his brother and sisters learned the meaning of the word discipline long before they could pronounce it. Their mother, Jimmy recalls, his attitude a combination of humor and awe, "was a pretty tough woman." He likes to think of her as the "frontier type," and in his childhood she was indeed close to that description both literally and figuratively, especially when it came to rearing children.

All of the children have memories of the razor strap. Its primary usage was not sharpening razors. And they were practically adult before they knew that castor oil had any purpose other than punishment.

Their mother was the type who *expected* certain things of her children. They were not rewarded for doing what was *expected* of them but punishment was swift and certain for not doing it.

For example, Jimmy was expected to return home promptly after school, change his clothes, do his chores, and remain in the yard unless or until his mother gave permission for him to leave. Now, should he dwaddle along to way, forget to change his clothes, not have time to do his chores, and run off to play, Whack! went the razor strap.

And, Jennetta was expected to clean up the kitchen after breakfast (when her mother left early for work), see to it that the younger children were propery dressed and off to school, and then go herself. Should her mother return from work to find that she did not get off to school, Ugh! out came the bottle of castor oil.

The razor strap was primarily, but not exclusively, for the boys. The castor oil was primarily, but not exclusively, for the girls.

The Hoffa children were *expected* to do well in school. Every evening after supper the table was cleared and the four of them gathered around the coal oil lamp with their books and tablets. Their mother took little or no part in this daily routine. Each child was on his own.

Jennetta, the oldest, and Nancy, the youngest, did best in their school work. Jimmy was on a demand schedule. He did his assignments as quickly as possible and that was that. Billy's academic prowess is better left undiscussed. Let us say that his intellectual inquisitivness was not fully manifest at this point.

Report card day was always eagerly anticipated by those who were doing well and dreaded by those who were not. Jennetta and Nancy couldn't wait to compare their grades with last month's and to get home to languish in their mother's unspoken but nonetheless recognizable praise.

For Jimmy the day was of no special consequence. He was an "average" student—perhaps high average—and although pride would not beam upon him from his mother's eyes, he was safe from admonishment or worse. For Billy report card day was often a bad time.

Jimmy and his sisters and brother were christened in the Christian Church at Brazil. They attended Sunday School regularly, learned to recite the Lord's Prayer and the Twenty-Third Psalm, and said their prayers at bedtime. None of the Hoffas talk much about religion.

* * * *

Grandpa Hoffa came to live with them when the family moved back to Vandalia Street, but his death followed John's in less than a year. Now there was little to hold Viola to Brazil and several good reasons for her to want to move to Clinton. First and most important, work was scarce in Brazil. Since John's passing she had taken in laundry, worked out at the big houses on The Hill, and cooked in a Main Street restaurant. Wherever she worked and whatever she did, the pay was poor. Clinton was a bigger town and a booming town. Secondly, she had many relatives living there for it was only a few miles from her girlhood community, Jessup. Her old friend Lizzie Guinn lived just across the State line in Illinois.

They left good and true friends in Stringtown, Brazil, Indiana: the Burns, the Brittons, the Riecherts, Lynches, Fergusons, Heads, Hughes, and the Frank Moores and the Jessee Moores, not to mention Grandpa Riddle and the Hoffa clan.

The Brittons lived next door. Harold, who was in his teens, often watched out for the Hoffa children when Viola was working away from home. His mother was a widow, too, and the families were close. They helped each other in sickness and in hard times.

Harold Britton reports an early display of the famous Jimmy Hoffa temper. He used to entertain the kids by pulling them in a wagon to the top of the hill and giving them a start down. Each had his turn. Once, he recalls, after doing this for an hour or so, he was so tired that he stopped about half way up the hill and told Jimmy to start from there. You took Billy all the way up and I'm as big as he, was Jimmy's unwavering position which he emphasized by yelling, pounding Harold's chest and stomach, and kicking his shins.

They rented a tiny two-room house that stood in the back yard of a slightly larger and grander house on Third Street in Clinton. It was a neighborhood of coal miners and laborers on a hilltop near the railroad tracks. The picture of coal blackened miners with red-rimmed eyes trudging up the hill from the tracks at the end of the day, carrying their lunch pails and leather plaited bull whips, etched itself on the ten-year-old brain of Jimmy Hoffa.

The rent for this house was six dollars per month. Jimmy and Billy were proud to bear the manly responsibility for delivering the money to the bank on the first day of each month. They rode double on an old bicycle that they had salvaged from the junk pile—this their fondest possession and most vivid memory of life in Clinton.

The principle family livelihood came from the "Hoffa home laundry." Every member of the family participated in this essential enterprise. Jimmy and Billy, their trusty wagon in tow, made the rounds to the homes of their customers to pick up bundles of dirty laundry. Theirs, too, was the responsibility of maintaining a fuel supply to fire the two great laundry tubs standing in the yard. They gathered windfalls from nearby wood lots and chopped new timber when this was necessary.

A hand cranked washing machine stood in the yard near the door in the summertime and on the porch or in the kitchen in winter. The boys took turns cranking while their mother fed wet wash through the wringer. The girls hung it out and gathered it in when it had dried. Sometimes the boys helped too. What a scramble when a sudden rain storm caught clothes on the line!

Viola did the ironing. Every housewife knows that this is tedious, time-consuming, back-breaking drudgery, but few have had the excruciating experience that Viola had of doing two or three family ironings a day several days a week.

Finally, Jimmy and Billy made the rounds delivering the finished laundry and collecting the money for it. The charge was one to two dollars for a family wash, depending on the size of the family, for the complete service; pick-up, washing, ironing, and delivery.

One day they were making a delivery of a heaped-high basket of freshly ironed laundry. A town bully, just for pure meanness, turned over wagon and basket into a dirty, coal-dusty, snow bank.

41

Jimmy looked at Billy and Billy looked at Jimmy. They knew without any discussion that they were in for a strapping when they got home with a basket of dirtied laundry that would have to be done all over again. Without one word spoken between them they reached the conclusion that since they were sure to "get it" they might as well have the satisfaction of dishing out the punishment due their antagonist. They did, and needless to say, that particular bully didn't bother them again. In fact, the word spread all over town that you couldn't fight one Hoffa boy without taking on both. Separately or together, they were tigers.

There were many times when the "home laundry" business simply was not enough to sustain the family. In periods of bad weather it might be a whole week before a washing could be finished. Viola tried to work in the homes of her customers as much as possible during the winter months. During one prolonged period she worked as an ironer at the Vermillion County Hospital, earning less than five dollars a day for this killing labor. At other times she worked as a cook and/or waitress in local restaurants. Life was very difficult for this sturdy woman. Perhaps the move to Clinton had been a mistake.

Jimmy, with characteristic resilience, took what came and managed to keep his puckish good humor through good times and bad. There is a wonderful snapshot of the family taken during this period. It shows Viola standing straight and stern beside Billy, who is looking past Nancy, Jennetta and Jimmy, directly into the lens of the camera. Nancy is very prim and proper and Jennetta would be too but for impish Jimmy who, at the moment the shutter snapped, tugged at her and said something that nobody remembers, his face contorted in sparkling fun.

Ever since John's passing Viola had lived hand to mouth never knowing for sure where the next day's work would come from and fearful that it might not come at all. The needs of four growing children were constant and unrestrained. They were like four little birds in a nest, open throats upturned, noisily awaiting the return of mother bird with a worm.

This lack of and frantic need for regular work and income forced Viola to leave the warmth of home country, old friends, and kin folks. Surely in a big city like Detroit she would find a steady job at set and certain wages. Just a pay envelope every week—it didn't have to be much—this was her vision of security.

They moved into the old West Side of Detroit in the neighborhood of Vinewood, Hubard, and Toledo Streets. They found a place to rent on Merritt Street. It had once been a single family dwelling and a rather fashionable one, too. But now it housed four families. The Hoffas had three rooms in the back downstairs.

The neighborhood hasn't changed much in forty years. Clark, Brandon, and McKinstry Streets—all are very clean as evidenced by neatly mown lawns, clipped hedges, and no garbage in sight. The houses are painted and freshly starched curtains adorn nearly every window.

It was, and generally remains, a community of Poles and Slavs with some Italians and Mexicans living on the outskirts. When the Hoffas came in 1924 they were among the first of the "hillbillies" from rural areas of the South and Midwest.

Grown men, of course, are forever recalling and chuckling about their boyhood battles which usually grow more numerous and rigorous with the passing years. But certainly this was a tough neighborhood. It is not hard to believe that the older residents greeted Jimmy and Billy with clenched fists instead of with open arms. However, it wasn't long before the Hoffa boys had established themselves.

They never looked for trouble and they never ran from it. They took care of themselves and if you fought one you had to fight the other. Jimmy and Billy, like the ancient Romans, preserved peace by their constant readiness for war.

When they left Clinton Viola sold or gave away or threw away the meager furniture in their possession. It wasn't worth shipping all the way to Detroit. Now she purchased the bare necessities on time, her brother cosigning the note. Obviously she had to have work at once.

She surveyed job possibilities and settled on one that she knew she could do satisfactorily. She took a job in a laundry as a clothes presser. She worked eight hours a day, five and a half days a week. She kept this job for three months while the family got settled in its new environment.

She heard that she could make more money working in a factory. Then she heard that they were hiring at Turnstead's, an automobile parts and accessory manufacturing company. The hitch was that they would take only those who had factory production line experience. Viola had never seen the inside of a factory. She sheepishly recalls that she fibbed on the experience and laughs when remembering the actual job she was called upon to perform. For eight hours every day she screwed a tap onto a bolt as it glided past her on the line. It was onery work but she stayed on at Turnstead's for four years. When she took a forced vacation due to an appendectomy she looked around just to see if by chance anything better was available. She took a job at the Fisher Body Fleetwood plant polishing the fancy radiator caps which in those days rivaled the door slam as quality indicators to new car buyers.

At various times when work was slack and especially during the deep depression years 1932-38, she worked in a bakery, in laundries, hospitals, and in different manufacturing plants. During one period she worked one day a week as a charwoman on the passenger boats of the Detroit and Cleveland Steamship Line. She continued to work right on up until 1948 when the children began supporting her.

When he was such a little fellow back in Brazil and Clinton work for Jimmy had been mostly play. He had done his chores every day with an eye on the razor strap and with no more resistance or enthusiasm than any small boy. Occasionally he had done a minor job for a neighbor for pay but pride and joy had overwhelmed any sensation of labor. No one who has not experienced it can imagine the feeling of sheer *goodness* that engulfs a child of a poor family when he hands to his mother money that he has earned completely on his own and without her suggestion or insistence. But when he was about eleven years old work began in earnest. He and his brother became serious contributors to the family livelihood.

Jimmy's work consisted of cleaning basements, carrying in coal and wood, and dumping out ashes. He earned pennies, nickles, and dimes and every cent was turned over to his mother. He worked after school and on Saturdays sacking potatoes at C. L. Smith's grocery store for the grand sum of fifty cents a week. He did odd jobs for many retail stores in the neighborhood, delivering groceries, passing out handbills, loading and unloading trucks, sweeping and cleaning.

The Hoffa children enrolled at the Frank C. Neinas School at the corner of Cavalry and McMillan Streets. They were advanced one grade due to the superiority of Indiana schools over those of Detroit. Together and separately they continued in the pattern set in earlier school days. Nancy, who had had the benefit of a private kindergarden and preschool coaching in Brazil now emerged as a typical little girl smarty pants. She was a straight A student and was pushed ahead into the class with Jimmy and Billy. They ignored her. Jennetta, a grade ahead, did good work. Jimmy did what was required of him and Billy dragged along.

Mrs. Hoffa was no less demanding than before. Every evening the table was cleared and they hovered over their books. She did not examine their assignments or homework. She only looked at the results when test papers were graded and report cards issued. They were *expected* to do well under penalty of the razor strap and the castor oil.

Jimmy was a reader. He read indiscriminately, haphazardly, but widely and thoroughly of everything that came his way. He liked reading assignments and therefore preferred history, English literature, and civics and government to arithmetic and science.

He hated to recite and sometimes would feign ignorance, even when he knew the subject well, to avoid having to stand and deliver in front of the class. But despite this reticence he earned a good reputation for retentive reading. Once he read something, it was said, he remembered it forever.

Jimmy did not like special attention. He never appeared in a school play, rarely misbehaved, and was never a teacher's pet.

In gym class he was slightly less reserved. He participated vigorously and won bronze, silver, and gold medals for the decathelon, and he represented his school in interscholastic meets.

Jimmy graduated from the ninth grade at Neinas School. He received a diploma and had his picture taken in front of the house with his chum, Nelson Gould. Both boys were combed, pressed, shined, and smiling in new double-breasted suits with knickerbockers. Billy got his diploma too. Their mother was very proud of them that day.

Jimmy worked steadily that summer. His main job was in a grocery store where he was stock boy, clean-up man, and errand boy all in one. In addition he did odd jobs around the neighborhood. Every week he brought money to his mother. Billy and Jennetta were working too and the family was in better shape financially than it had been at any time within his memory of such things.

As the summer drew to a close he thought more and more, and more and more seriously, about quitting school for good. He discussed it with his mother many times and at last she told him to make up his own mind.

When the new term began he went to Western High School to enroll. He sat there for a while awaiting his turn. Memories of the lean years since his father's death were flashing through his mind. He remembered the days of the "Hoffa home laundry" when they had lived dollar-to-dollar and day-to-day; when a rainy day would upset the family economy and a whole week of bad weather meant disaster. He knew the struggles his mother had endured to find and keep steady employment and uninterrupted income. He was painfully aware of the frustrating, infuriating despair of having to get along week after week, month after month, on not quite enough.

At fourteen Jimmy had had enough poverty to last the rest of his life. Working and earning agreed with him. Before they came to his name on the enrollment list he got up and left, thus ending the formal education of Jimmy Hoffa.

* * * *

Not long after his decision to drop out of school his mother heard about an opening for a boy in a downtown department store. She went with him to apply for the job. There was a brief, informal interview as Jimmy was looked over and sized up. The most important question seemed to be whether he possessed a jacket that would make him presentable to customers. He had the coat to the new suit that Mom had bought for his graduation. They asked how long it would take for him to get it. Twenty minutes later he was back at the store reporting for his first day's work.

The name of the store was Frank & Cedar's. Jimmy worked there two years as a stock boy. His work brought him out among the customers and occasionally when they were particularly rushed he was allowed to wait on a shopper.

Jimmy worked hard and conscientiously. Hours were long and pay was meager but he was proud of his job and felt himself lucky to have it. Without even a second thought about it he turned over to his mother all the money he earned. She returned what he needed for carfare, lunches, and other personal expenses.

Jimmy was by nature as well as upbringing a frugal boy. For example, he often hitched a ride to and from work on the rear end of the trolley car, ducking down low to escape the motorman's line of vision. Of greater importance from the standpoint of economy, he rarely participated in recreational activities that entailed expenses. He did not have dates. He did not often go to the movies. He liked sports, but more as a participant than a spectator. Fishing and reading were his main hobbies and he fished in public waters with homemade tackle, and he read newspapers, second-hand books and magazines acquired by swapping around the neighbohood, and books from the public library.

Clothing was not a big item in the family budget when the children were very young. But as they grew older and attended school, their mother was uncommonly insistent and watchful about their dress and personal appearance. Jimmy's school clothes usually consisted of a clean cotton shirt worn under a sweater or jacket or both in cold weather, woolen knickers that buckled just below the knee, high socks, shoes, and cap. He was under standing orders to come home immediately after school and to change clothes at once.

His "every day" outfit, for after school and on Saturdays and holidays, was bib-type overalls, cotton "work" shirt, and tennis shoes. Long underwear and shoes were optional after May 15 and Jimmy never failed to exercise his option to shed them.

After he went to work at Frank & Cedar's, two factors combined to make Jimmy more clothes conscious and to upgrade their quality and quantity. He had to dress reasonably well to meet store requirements and his mother took advantage of his employee's discount in purchasing new clothes for him. The result was that Jimmy was considered a very well dressed young man.

Jimmy's social life was pretty much confined to the family circle. They celebrated birthdays in the traditional family way. Mom baked a cake and decorated it with the appropriate number of candles and after the wishing and blowing she led the children in singing "Happy Birthday to You" to the lucky one and presents were given. Thanksgiving was a time of feasting with turkey and all the trimmings, plus Mom's delicious pies and cakes. On the Fourth of July firecrackers and flags were completely in order.

Christmas, too, was a happy family occasion. The boys went into the nearest woods to search for the prettiest, best-shaped evergreen tree which was set up in the front room. For days in advance the children hurried through their homework so as to have time in the evening to pop and string popcorn, to string cranberries, and to make pretty colored paper ornaments for hanging on the tree. Mom made cookies, candy, cakes and pies. Even in the leanest years Christmas was a happy time. Santa Claus never failed them and the children always had presents for Mom.

Jimmy did not pay much attention to girls during his

teen-aged years. There were plenty of them around the neighborhood and the Hoffa household. Mrs. Hoffa neither encouraged nor discouraged his interest in the opposite sex. When occasionally a neigborhood girl went out of her way to notice him, she was ignored for her trouble.

CHAPTER 4

The
Strawberry
Affair

"Move! HOFFA! Move!"

"The rest of you—Collins, Calhoun, Langley, Holmes— All of you! Get the lead out and get them crates into the warehouse. MOVE! MOVE!"

The men muttered short, ugly words and phrases through clenched teeth.

"You little bastard. You'll get yours."

"Go to hell, Banty Legs."

The soothing voice of Sam Calhoun cut through the rumble. "Knock it off Bobby. Can it, Jimmy. That stuff won't get you nowhere."

It was 11:00 p.m. at Kroger's produce warehouse. Men and boys formed a human conveyor belt. Back and forth they shuffled. They had been on the job since 5:00 p.m. During the first half of the long night they unloaded fresh produce from the ice-cooled boxcars that arrived at the rail siding, stacking the crates neatly in the depths of the night-cooled warehouse. Sometime after midnight they would begin assembling orders for the retail Kroger grocery stores, loading the same produce into the bodies of delivery trucks. In between boxcars to unload or trucks to load they sat around on the steps outside, if it was summer, or clustered around a big coal stove inside, if it was winter. The pay was thirty-two cents an hour for actual time worked. A man might earn fifteen dollars in a good week although he had to be on the job sixty, seventy, or even eighty hours to do it counting the time in between work periods.

Jimmy quit his job at Frank & Cedar's department store because he wanted and needed a man's job at man's pay. As a stockboy he had earned only ten dollars a week and no promotion was in sight. He worked like a dog and his bosses liked him. "You've got a bright future here, young man," they told him. But Jimmy couldn't wait for the future. He started out to meet it.

As a schoolboy he had worked after school, Saturdays, and during summer vacations at neighborhood Kroger grocery stores. The main offices and warehouses of the huge chain were only a few blocks from the Hoffa home on Scotten Street and many friends and acquaintances worked there. Even though the times were tough and unemployment was high, with so many connections and recommendations going for him, Jimmy had no trouble getting a job.

Maybe it was predestined. Who can say? But it is difficult to think that the events and circumstances of his seventeen years, pulling, shoving, and knocking against each other, bringing him to this particular place, at this particular time, and in a particular frame of mind, could have been mere chance. It could have been God's work, or the devil's. He was at seventeen a complex, fathomless mixture of seemingly conflicting characteristics.

Deeply conscious of and attentive to the material needs of his family, he was undemonstrative to the point of indifference to them in personal relationships. He was invariably the hardest worker on a job, but work held no fascination, satisfaction, nor even interest for him. He liked girls but was too shy, too disdainful, or too preoccupied; it is not clear which; to take advantage of any romantic opportunities that came his way.

His clothes were clean and well-kept, carelessely worn. His appetite was big and hearty, without strong preferences in food or drink. He disliked attention, but inevitably attracted it. He was cheerful, but not happy.

Young Jimmy Hoffa viewed the world about him through calm eyes; watched, absorbed, waited.

Jimmy had friends at the warehouse before he went to work there and found new ones on the job. Bobby Holmes, Frank Collins, Sam Calhoun, Jay Langley, and Jimmy were on the same shift. Holmes had come to America from England two years earlier "to get out of the mines." Collins was a product of Detroit's West Side. Langley was a "Hillbilly" like Jimmy. He had followed the Hoffas from Indiana partly if not solely on account of his personal interest in Jennetta, whom he later married. Sam Calhoun, at thirty-three, a quiet, thoughtful man more mature than his years, was the old man of the quintet. He had had trade union experience as an employee of the Railway Express Agency. He was union-minded and he talked union to his friends. Perhaps he more than anyone else within or without the group deserves the credit or blame (depending on the point of view) for Jimmy Hoffa's early entry into unionism.

Al Hastings, Jimmy was to say years later, "Was the kind of guy who causes labor unions." He was the "pusher" in charge of the night shift at the produce warehouse. He was a short, stocky man with bowed and skinny legs. He had the temperament of a top sergeant and the voice to match. The men knew what to do, so when he screamed, often using profanity, it was not to direct them but solely to keep them going at top speed. He was such a little man (they always are) that he stood on a raised platform to oversee and overshout the men.

Hastings did not have authority to fire but his recommendation went a long way with the warehouse superintendent, Mr. Blough. In the end he fired Jimmy and made it stick. We shall get to that.

Working conditions at the warehouse were bad by the standards of 1930 and deplorable by today's. Although the men had to be on the job twelve hours or more to get paid for six or eight hours, that wasn't the worst of it. The thing that really galled them was the complete lack of job security.

The great depression came early and with devastating severity to Detroit. In those harsh times business was rotten and gangs of unemployed men and women hung around factory gates and loading docks hoping and praying for a day's or an hour's work. Everywhere that men worked, other men stood by, reduced by the degrading forces of the times to human vultures waiting to pounce on any morsel of work.

At the Kroger warehouse when a man quit or was fired or left the job for any reason, even a family or personal emergency, Al Hastings would step outside and beckon. His slightest signal would summon scores of idle onlookers who waited days for just such opportunities. Hastings would look them over like a drill sergeant inspecting raw recruits, poking and proding with his eyes and asking insulting questions. He would wring every drop of drama out of the hiring process before majestically making his selection on the basis of his personal preference, prejudices, and whim.

As though they didn't know it, Hastings took pains to remind the regular workers of the brimming reservoir of surplus labor awaiting his call. His frequent tirades were sprinkled with such encouraging comments as: "If you don't want to work there's plenty outside that do!" Or: "You bums gonna load that truck or do I have to go outside?"

His delight in these harangues, it seemed to Jimmy and his friends, was surpassed only by his orgasmic pleasure in firing somebody, making it stick, and going through his strut in the hiring process.

As the nights warmed and shortened for summer so did Al Hastings' temper. The slightest breach of the un-written and ill-defined work rules was sufficient to earn summary dismissal subject only to the rather hopeless prospect that Mr. Blough might reverse the decision. This rarely happened, especially during this season. Several men were sure to be fired on one pretense or another to make room on the payroll for summertime—schoolboy —employees. These were the sons, nephews, and friends of company big-shots. Some worked to pay college tuition and some just for the experience and pin-money. But no circumstances made it justifiable to the men whose jobs were jeopardized or lost. Weighing their own needs; food, shelter, and clothing; against the needs of the summer employees; college tuition, experience, and pin-money; their frustration turned to desperation and anger.

With their many unpaid rest periods during the long nights the men had ample time to dwell upon, perhaps to enlarge upon, their many grievances. Most of them grumbled aimlessly. But the five friends, Hoffa, Calhoun, Holmes, Collins, and Langley, slowly pieced together a plan to try to do something about conditions. They met during every break, hashing and re-hashing their thoughts.

This was the era of the open shop, the lock out, and the strike breaker. The men in the warehouse knew what they had at risk, namely, their jobs. They could hear Al Hastings now: "Okay you ungrateful bastards, get out of here. Make room for men who appreciate a job." They knew, too, that the company could, and no doubt would, bring in a platoon or a company of back alley toughs, however many might be necessary, armed with policemen's billys, to throw them out if they didn't leave voluntarily. And they knew that Detroit city police would be on the streets ready to work them over once more if they didn't move on fast enough. All this could happen in a matter of hours and the company then would roll on like old man river and the men would join the ranks of the unemployed. Such visions inured caution among the conspirators. They had to come up with something more than mere confrontation, and they did.

"We gotta pull it off when a carload of expensive stuff is in the siding," Calhoun counseled, "Hit 'em in the pocketbook." And one thing more, and this was Holmes' idea: "We don't want to ask for too much. Let's make it easy for 'em." With these tactics firmly agreed to the five schemers set out to get firm commitments from the other men.

"So damn much was wrong," Bobby Holmes related. "We made lists, divided them up, and systematically talked to every man in the warehouse, appealing to each on an individual basis, on the basis of what we thought or knew he would be most sympathetic to. If a guy had a run-in with Al Hastings one of us was sure to get to him during the next break. If a man was short changed in the work assignments, we talked to him about getting a guarantee on so much work per week. If a man had a friend who had been fired for nothing, we talked to him about that. We tried to find every man's soft spot. It took a long time. Gradually we got a majority behind us and we figured the rest would go along when the chips were down, but we weren't as sure as we thought we ought to be."

In April, 1931 an incident occured which solidified the men in their determination to "do something." Two men left the job for a midnight luncheon, which was customary, but while they were out Al Hastings hired replacements. They returned to be informed that they were no longer employees of the Kroger company. That did it. Practically every man of the 175 warehouse employees was ready to strike. Calhoun called a meeting of the five leaders and they agreed that the time had come to make their move.

A few days later a carload of fresh strawberries arrived at the warehouse. They had to be transferred immediately to trucks for delivery to the retail stores. "Strawberries die very quickly so we waited until the trucks were about half loaded then we stopped and walked away," Holmes told. The workers assembled on the loading dock, 175 strong, confronting Hastings who was almost out of his mind. He cursed and shouted, threatening them individually and collectively. "This is private property," he repeated over and over, "either you get to work or get the hell out!" The men ignored his ranting and waited for leadership.

Calhoun, Hoffa, Holmes, Collins, and Langley converged through the crowd, soothing and calming the men. "Get Blough," Calhoun curtly ordered Hastings, but the "pusher" responded by renewing his own orders to the men to get back to work or off of the platform. Soon the men began to chant, "We want Blough! We want Blough! To hell with you, Banty Legs. We're through with you, you little s.o.b. Blough! Blough! Blough! BLOUGH!"

While Hastings was trying to be heard above the din, Mr. Blough came out of his office to see what was going on. He knew in an instant.

It was a brief negotiating session. With one eye on the rapidly perishing strawberries Mr. Blough quickly agreed to talk with the leaders tomorrow if the men would finish the job tonight.

Few of the men realized it, but when they went back to work they were a union. "But we didn't start out to organize a union," Bobby Holmes said. "In fact, we had a number of organizers come around in those days and we always gave them the cold shoulder. We were young and we listened to all of them, but we were afraid to turn ourselves over to outside leadership. We thought we could do better for ourselves if we kept our independence.

"We were just a group of hard-up people trying to better ourselves in the only way we knew how. We were trying to nail down our jobs and we were hoping in the long run to get higher pay."

Perhaps their innocence won for them. Under the circumstances, Mr. Blough was not dealing with a union *per se*. He was dealing with his employees. Like many employers, then and now, he felt that he could handle things and keep his people happy so long as no union was involved.

Hoffa, Holmes, Calhoun, Langley, and Collins sat in on the promised meeting with Mr. Blough and other company officials. Calhoun was their spokesman. Their biggest gripe, the lack of job security, was the first and main topic. In this and subsequent meetings they developed a set of standards and an understanding regarding this vital issue. In addition, they gained minor concessions on work rules—lunch breaks, wash room facilities, smoking—little things which taken separately seem petty but which, when taken in the aggregate, add up to the difference between misery and reasonable contentment on a job. Al Hastings was still the boss but the men knew where they stood on many of his hitherto pet and unpredictable peeves. In the future he would at least have to justify his petty picking on them.

What was Jimmy's role in these events? In the beginning his assignments befitted his status as the youngest member of the leadership group. He was the eager-beaver errand boy, rounding up the fellows for meetings, delivering messages between them, going out for coffee and doughnuts, and serving as lookout-for-Al Hastings when they had their heads together. His own recollections of this era are scanty for he is a man who seldom reflects on the past. When asked what motivated him to throw himself so wholeheartedly into union work at such an early age, this was his reply:

"I would think that poverty and having to work too many hours on the job to make a living. I grew up in a real poor neighborhood. My mother worked for 17 cents an hour. I got 50 cents a week sacking potatoes after school and all day Saturday. I passed out hand bills for a quarter a day and you worked all day. And then there's the question of having absolute control of men on a job, a guy named Al Hastings, a little bit of a guy. He was an animal—threw things at them and cursed them all night. He delighted to see people get hurt. He was the cause of us organizing Kroger's."

In the last days before the strawberry strike Jimmy displayed uncanny ability in enlisting the support of his fellow workers. He was a born organizer. William Crow, one of his earliest recruits, said: "He stood right close up to you and looked right at you. He can really look at you. His face was, well, open. He was the sincere-est little guy I've ever seen. He gave me confidence. Up to then I'd been scared to join a union but Jimmy made me feel that it was just the right thing to do."

Calhoun took particular notice of Jimmy's skill. Immediately after the strawberry incident when it became apparent that some sort of formal, permanent organization was needed, Calhoun, who was elected president by acclamation, saw to it that Jimmy was elected vice president. Holmes became secretary-treasurer—"without treasure," he recalls.

Jimmy did a lot of growing up during the next eighteen months. Indeed, it was the beginning of his maturity in that for the first time he found, in the union movement, something beyond the raw elements of survival to interest him. He did not, however, think of it in philosophical terms. He only knew that there was great opportunity in doing things to get more money and more job security for working people. (To this day, Jimmy would be the last to deny that he is a thorough-going opportunist.) He threw himself into union work.

During these troubled times Detroit was a hotbed of labor unrest. "It was the open-shop capital of the world," Jimmy says. "Every time you went near a place to organize you'd get picked up and put in jail. The police beat you on the head with night-sticks. It was a mess. We fought on the streets. The employers hired every hoodlum strike-breaker in town. We used to laugh to see the police and the ex-cons lined up together against us."

Jimmy worked at Kroger's nights and for the union days. Slowly but surely a bona fide union took form. They printed up membership cards, rented an office of sorts, and bought an old roll-top desk for $20 which they raised "by popular subscription"—in other words, they chipped in.

In the produce business celery was packed twelve bunches to a crate although it was ordered by the retail stores in units of six bunches. It was easy enough for a warehouseman to open a crate in an orthodox way, but it was even easier, and it was also the mark of an experienced man, to drop it in just such a certain way and it would pop open. Al Hastings kept an eye open and an ear cocked for a breaking celery crate. It was a firing offense because it bruised and therefore hastened spoilage of the vegetable.

Hastings watched him like a hawk anyway, and when Jimmy got a little cocky, careless, or fed up, and it might have been any of the three or a combination of them, he let a crate drop and Al was right on top of him. They exchanged unflattering appraisals of each other and thus and then ended Jimmy's career with the Kroger company.

In the meantime their independent union had seen fit

to affiliate with the Teamsters' Union and young Jimmy Hoffa's organizing genius had become the talk of Joint Council 43, the top-ranking Teamster unit in the area. Martin Haggerty, an International Organizer, which is a very prestigeous position in the Teamsters' hierarchy, was instrumental in making a place for him on the Joint Council staff. There was no salary. Organizers were paid on a commission basis—so much for each new member.

While Jimmy progressed rapidly in a man's world, gaining the respect and deference of his elders, he remained a boy in many ways. He still lived at home under the iron will and discipline of his mother. He took his pay envelope home to her and received funds to cover his personal expenses. And he sought her counsel on important matters as late as when he made the decision to go to work full-time for Joint Council 43. Characteristically, Mrs. Hoffa listened patiently and encouraged him to consider every aspect and not to make a hasty decision, but in the end advised him to make his own decision.

He was Spartan in his personal habits, neither drinking, smoking, nor loafing around pool halls or street corners. He tasted beer once or twice but didn't like it. It is told that he took a glass of wine with a meal and became violently ill. He was a man of physical activity in the tradition of Theodore Roosevelt—no sailing, skiing, touch football for him—his idea of sport was hiking in the woods, hunting, fishing, horseback riding, and gymnastics.

He had a lingering boyish joy about such things as riding the rides at fairs and carnivals; the roller coaster, the whip, and that thing that holds you straight up and upside down. He enjoyed baiting and cajoling timid friends to go along with him. He loved firecrackers. On the Fourth of July he would stroll down the street happily lighting and throwing two-inchers to either side.

Jimmy had a girl. Her name was Eileen. But while she

heard wedding bells in the distance, Jimmy heard only factory whistles, time clocks dinging, and the grinding gears of a tractor-trailer rig. In time Eileen drifted away and Jimmy continued and intensified his love affair with organized labor; his flirtation with power—his only mistress.

CHAPTER 5

Song of the Teamsters' Union

Jimmy Hoffa moved into an executive position with the Teamsters' Union at 21 when he was appointed business agent of Local 299, a run-down, debt-ridden, poorly organized unit of some two hundred and fifty disinterested members. He set out with characteristic vigor to make something out of his new job.

He found opportunity in the turbulent times. The depression was going full blast, and, according to Jimmy: "No where in the country did you find a situation like Detroit. It was almost a revolution. It could have been a bloody revolution. People were living in parks and eating out of garbage cans. They were hungry and they were mad. They didn't know what they were mad at but they were looking for something. The town was full of radicals and commies trying to stir them up and they could get a crowd any time. It was the most distressed city in the country and nobody was doing anything about it."

Jimmy waded into the mess with only one thing on his mind; to build up Local 299. His philosophical views came later. At the time his motive was more pragmatic. He was supposed to be making twenty-five dollars a week but the union bank account was overdrawn when he took over. He had to hustle to get new members who brought with them initiation fees and dues. Many weeks during his first months he took home only five or ten dollars.

This personal incentive pushed Jimmy all over the place. Anyone who drove a truck or worked in a warehouse was fair game. Soon even these broad restrictions were by-passed. Hoffa was everywhere.

He kept dozens of projects going at a time, like so many balls juggling in mid-air. Starting at seven in the morning his day was spent almost solely in organizing activities. He might begin on a loading dock, button-holing warehousemen as they came on the job. Next he would talk to the drivers as they loaded their trucks. One of his selling points was the prospect that someday they would sit in the cab while warehousemen did the loading.

Before noon he would have spent an hour at the office, there to take and receive telephone calls and calls in person from his shop stewards and other union men in the field. The afternoon would find him on a picket line, and more organizing. There was sure to be at least one meeting at night. It might be an organizing rally, a negotiating session with employers, or internal union business.

He took a few lumps in the course of these activities. Employers were not exactly thrilled when they got the word that a union organizer was on the loading dock. As Jimmy's reputation grew they were especially disenchanted by his presence. They would politely ask him to leave, like; "Get the hell out of here or I'll bust your head!", and a couple of goons riding shot-gun for the boss would grimace menacingly for emphasis. This was all part of the game for a union organizer in the 1930's.

"In the early days you couldn't even get recognition without a strike," Jimmy said, "and every strike was a fight. Usually we kept the picket lines going day and night, sleeping in cars or on the ground. The strikebreakers tried to run us away and the police helped them.

"I was in a lot of fights. I got my head busted a few times and I tried to give as good as I got. My brother got shot by a strikebreaker. One of our business agents was killed."

Jimmy was picked up by the police more times than he can remember: "Once I was taken to jail 18 times within 24 hours. Every time I showed up on the picket line I got thrown into jail. The sergeant would say, 'What are you doing here?' I'd say, 'What do you think?' He took me downtown. The captain asked what I had done. 'Nothing,' I said. They let me go and right back to the picket line I went. The sergeant followed and picked me up again. When he got me downtown he told the captain, 'He was going to cause trouble.' This went on all day and all night."

Hoffa was arrested a number of times during the 1930's. He was convicted three times but never served any time. One conviction came on an assault and battery charge. It was a picket line fight and Jimmy "gave as good as he got."

Another conviction resulted from an anti-trust violation. It seems that Jimmy invented a new organizing technique. Apparently he went to some waste paper companies (or they came to him) and made a deal. They helped sign up their employees for membership in the Teamsters' Union, and in return the union used pressure and the picket line to prevent competition by non-unionized companies. The court took a dim view of this convenient arrangement.

A third conviction resulted from charges that he forced grocery stores to buy permits from the union. Jimmy denied vehemently that he would stoop to such nonsense, but the court found differently.

But Jimmy readily admits "I'm no angel." Indeed, he has a low opinion of labor leaders of that era who didn't get in a few fracases with the law. "A union organizer who didn't get in trouble with the police was either buying them off or he wasn't doing his job," he growls.

Jimmy used every known organizing technique and invented a few new ones. Sometimes he organized from the bottom up, so to speak, recruiting individual employees until he had enough manpower to confront the boss with the ultimatum: recognition or strike. Sometimes he organized from within, quietly signing up key employees who then induced their fellow employees to come along. And sometimes he organized from the top down, winning or coercing management first and then letting the boss himself do the honors of enlisting his employees into the union. Jimmy developed tremendous talent for playing one employer against another, but by no means, as in the case of the waste paper companies, illegally. And he wasn't averse to taking on another union in internecine warfare for members. Some of his methods are now illegal but Jimmy took full advantage of them when they were legal.

While he was still working as an organizer on the staff of Joint Council 43 a drive was begun that was to lay the foundation of Jimmy's future. This project was to organize the truckaway, driveaway, and car hauler workers —the men who delivered new cars from Detroit to dealers' show rooms throughout the nation. The task was made difficult by two factors. First, the drivers were not only apathetic and afraid for their jobs, but they were virtually inaccessable due to frequent, almost constant, absence from the Detroit area. Secondly, the employers fought back with the cleverness and ferocity of Lee defending Richmond.

Jimmy did not initiate this project but his ingenuity and energy carried it to its ultimate successful conclusion. He overcame the problem of meeting the drivers face-to-face by stalking them on the highways. In those days there were few truck terminals with facilities for drivers. When a man got too sleepy to go on he just pulled over to the side and got as comfortable as possible in the cab of his truck. Jimmy would drive along a highway until he came upon a sleeping truck driver, stop, wake him up, and make his pitch for the Teamsters' Union. Many an old timer remembers these encounters.

"I was about half way between Detroit and Cleveland," Woodrow Sylvester recalls. "Guess I'd been sawing the wood for about twenty minutes when the door opening woke me up. I was still half asleep. This little guy looked up at me, grinning. I thought he was a bum looking for a ride. But he said, 'My name is Hoffa. Can I talk with you about the Teamsters?' I said, 'No you can't. Now get out of here and let me sleep.' He said, 'Just five minutes; that's all I ask.' Well, I was awake anyhow so I told him to go ahead."

Jimmy was well-informed, clever, and tireless. And once he got his foot in the door he didn't give up easily. Woody Sylvester continued: "He really bore in on me. I told him I was scared I'd get fired if I joined a union. He said by the time I got back to Detroit everybody would have joined. I told him I couldn't afford the dues. He said if we got organized I'd make it up in pay raises and more besides. I told him I didn't like unions anyhow. Them union guys was always causing trouble. He said in the Teamsters' Union I would be invited to all the meetings and the members called the shots. He had an answer for everything and he never let up. If I hadn't signed that membership card we'd still be there."

Jimmy's technique worked. Soon Martin Haggerty, Al Squires, and other organizers adopted it and fanned out from Detroit. They were making headway when the employers began to catch on and fight back. Their counter technique was strictly strong-arm. They sent tough strikebreakers along with the regular driver. When an organizer poked his head into a truck he was likely as not to get a mouthful of knuckles for his trouble. Some union men claimed that the companies sent out decoy trucks manned by muscle men. The battle raged on for years but in the end the Teamsters won. Today this group of workers forms a special division of the International Brotherhood of Teamsters and James Hoffa heads it.

Many successful men have a knack for jumping on the right bandwagon or being in the right place at the right time, or so it seems to less successful onlookers. During these years another Teamster organizing project was getting underway and as fortune would have it Jimmy was eventually propelled right into the middle of it.

In Minneapolis three brothers, Vince, Miles, and Grant Dunne, a bright young organizer named Farrell Dobbs, and a tough ex-lumberjack and railroad worker named Karl Skoglund, successfully conducted an intensive organizational drive which resulted in a very strong Teamsters' Local with practically all truck drivers in the city as members. With this formidable base of power they then set out to bring into the fold the over-the-road drivers, not only those headquartered in Minneapolis, but the entire Northwest.

This ambitious project was the brain-child of Farrell Dobbs, whom Jimmy hails to this day as a "very far-sighted individual . . . the draftsman and architect of our road operations."

Dobbs felt that organizing the over-the-road drivers was vital because "miserable working conditions among any group of drivers is a potential threat to better working conditions among other drivers." Also, Dobbs, who was very political-minded, saw the long distance drivers as potential missionaries carrying the gospel of trade unionism to the remotest corners of the country. They would spread the good news, he believed, by word and by example.

Dobbs did not have the wholehearted backing of higher-ups in the International Brotherhood of Teamsters, Dan Tobin, General President of the IBT, thought the over-the-road drivers were just so much "trash", not good enough for his high-minded union. Several influential Teamster chieftains opposed the project, too. They, too, forsaw that the over-the-road drivers might become missionaries and they wanted no proselyting in their particular jungles. However, in time Dobbs won enough support to win the hesitant approval of Dan Tobin and the Executive Board. Among his most ardent backers was Red O'Laughlin, the top-ranking Teamster of Detroit. When they had conferences to discuss and plan the operation O'Laughlin brought along Jimmy Hoffa. "I did a lot of listening at those meetings," Jimmy recalls, "When they asked me something I'd answer the best I could but, except for that, I kept my mouth shut.

As a matter of fact, Jimmy was among a handful of organizers who had experience in recruiting long-distance drivers. No doubt Red O'Laughlin was mindful of this when he took him to the meetings in Minneapolis and when, later he farmed him out to Farrell Dobbs to directly assist in the organizing campaign. The techniques Jimmy had developed to such a fine edge while organizing the truckaway and driveaway drivers were adopted in a body by Dobbs.

The Dunne brothers, by the way, soon faded out of the picture. They were known "Trotskyites," that is, Communists who adhered to the teachings of Trotsky as opposed to those of Lenin. In the 1930's to be a Communist was not so unthinkable as it became after World War II. But nevertheless the Teamsters' Union was strongly anti-communist even then. Dan Tobin called on his friend President Franklin D. Roosevelt for help and by applying the anti-communist Smith Act, the Dunnes and other Communists were thrown out of the IBT. Some ex-Communists who were close to the Dunne brothers claim, with some bitterness, that Hoffa had a hand in flushing them out but Jimmy, who would be proud to take the credit, disclaims it. He was sent to Minneapolis strictly for organizing purposes and nothing more.

In January, 1937, representatives of thirteen Locals in the Dakotas, Iowa, Minnesota, Wisconsin, and Michigan met with Farrell Dobbs and formed the North Central District Drivers Council. It remained for the organizers, including Jimmy Hoffa, to put meat and muscle, in the form of membership, on the bare bones of the organization hidden by that impressive title. Within about one year the Council had grown to include forty-six locals in eleven States. Dobbs felt strong enough to confront the trucking companies with the ambitious goal of the Council: "To establish uniform wages, hours, and working conditions for all truck drivers in the eleven State area."

It wasn't easy merely to confront the truck operators due to the nature of the industry, which was everywhere and nowhere. There were a few big operators but many hundreds of small-scale truckers, including thousands of owner-operators, in the area. The union's Area Negotiating Committee submitted its demands to the American Trucking Association but that organization refused to be drawn into negotiations on grounds that it had no jurisdiction to act on behalf of the employers.

Dobbs' fertile mind had long since grasped that the greatest vulnerability of the trucking industry from the trade unionists point of view lay in the scattered, yet interlocked and interdependent, nature of its operations. The very essense of the business is mutual back-scratching among the separate operators. There are four broad categories of operations: local cartage, transfer and storage, pickup and delivery, and over-the-road. They serve and service each other. For example, the pickup and delivery operator will deliver goods to a terminal where the over-the-road trucker reloads it for the long haul to the city of its destination. Obviously, a work stoppage among pick-up and delivery operators has an instant effect upon the over-the-road operators, not only those locally domiciled, but over a wide area, perhaps several States. A tie up of trucking in a key terminal city usually generates pressures upon employers *by* employers.

In this instance Dobbs decided to make Chicago the first pressure point. It didn't take long to get down to business. A strike was not necessary. As soon as the employers realized that the Teamsters really meant business they formed an Operator's Committee to meet the union's Area Negotiating Committee.

Dobbs' strategy in selecting Chicago as the kicking off point paid handsome dividends. It was a key terminal for the entire mid-West. Many truckers from surrounding States wanted to be in on the negotiations which were sure to affect their future operations. The two committees got down to business and after many long and arduous bargaining sessions an agreement was reached.

The agreement called for uniform wage scales and working conditions throughout the eleven-State area. Sixty percent of the union men involved got pay raises at once. A minimum wage set just below the hourly rate then being received by the highest paid workers. Drivers who owned their own trucks henceforth would be paid separately for their time and for their equipment. A formula was worked out for paying per-mile drivers for time spent loading and unloading and other delays. And finally, machinery was set up to assure compliance with the agreement uniformly everywhere in the area. A grievance committee was created with Farrell Dobbs as chairman.

In arriving at this historical agreement which for the

first time sought and achieved uniform wages, hours, and working conditions for drivers within a given, large, area, the union found friends among many far-sighted employers. Rate cutting, cost differentials due to wage differentials, and general labor unrest kept the industry in turmoil. Many employers felt (correctly, as time proved) that the uniformity asked by the Teamsters would serve to bring order in the chaotic business to the ultimate benefit of everybody concerned including the public.

However, the employers who had signed the agreement at Chicago were just the big boys. It remained to get general agreement among the hundreds of smaller trucking companies and owner-operators in the vast eleven-State area. Some bitter battles were fought. The worst of these was in Omaha where, due to local labor laws, the union was very weak. First the employers shut out the workers, then the union marshalled its Omaha members and brought in some outsiders to lend a hand, and finally a bitter, violent strike took place. Anti-picketing ordinances made it impossible for the union to stage an effective strike but once more Dobbs developed a winning strategy.

Bearing in mind the interdependent nature of the industry, Dobbs figured out that pressure on the truckers in Kansas City would force the surrender of those in Omaha due to the carriers' route structure and the flow of commerce between the two cities. "You push the button in Kansas City and Omaha jumps," Jimmy describes it. The union soon applied sufficient pressure to virtually isolate Omaha economically, so far as the trucking business was concerned. Omaha had to fall, and it did. The North Central District Drivers Council was a success.

During those fast-moving times Farrell Dobbs didn't pay much attention to Jimmy Hoffa, still a kid in his early 20's, but Jimmy paid close attention to him. He was quick to perceive the potential power of a network of vigorous Teamsters' Locals connected, both figuratively and literally, by the over-the-road drivers. He saw, too, the unlimited strategic advantages of the pressure and leverage techniques employed by Dodds and he realized that the successful application of these methods depended on having a thorough knowledge of the trucking industry. This was impressed upon him by the observation of Dobbs' master stroke in selecting Chicago as the place to start, and in choosing Kansas City as the pressure point for Omaha.

Jimmy learned the strategy of going from one major terminal city to another, coming back later to mop up the territory in between. This "leapfrog" technique, he realized, applied equally as well in negotiations and organizing. He saw that a strong over-the-road Local could be like the backbone of a fish, leading out to potential members in related industries. "Once you have the road men, you can get the local cartage, and once you have the local cartage, you can get anyone you want," Jimmy has said and proved.

The North Central District Drivers Council expanded geographically and gained membership steadily. In time its name was changed to Central States Drivers Council. In time Jimmy became its president. He is today its vice president and negotiating chairman, and its titular head. It is considered a main source of his tremendous power in the union and in the nation.

His experience in the over-the-road organizing campaign gave him additional maturity and confidence, and he gained valuable personal contacts within the IBT. It was the jumping off place of his subsequent rise to the top.

He was elected president of Local 299 in 1937. No longer the floundering, debt-ridden skeleton it had been when he took over as its business agent, it had 4,000 members and money in the bank, but this was just the beginning. Jimmy now began to apply to strictly local organizing all the techniques he had learned from Farrell Dobbs, who, incidently, had dropped out of the union movement to devote full time to his first love, politics.

Jimmy's super-aggressive organizing campaigns became the talk of union men everywhere. He concentrated for the time being on local cartage, bakery, laundry, and soft drink drivers. Frequently his zeal resulted in members for other unions, too. For example, he might strike a laundry, tieing up the whole operation, of course, just to organize for the Teamsters a dozen or so drivers. In the meantime the other laundry workers would sign up for the regular laundry workers' union.

In jurisdictional disputes between the competing American Federation of Labor (AFL), with which the Teamsters' Union was affiliated, and the Congress of Industrial Organizations (CIO), Local 299 played an active role. Indeed, Jimmy's local became known as the "fists" of the labor movement in Detroit. True, Jimmy was not afraid to use power persuasion, but more often he used his head.

For example, there is a clear record of Jimmy's role in the Detroit Street Railway dispute in 1941. The Detroit Free Press of August 25, 1941 credits him with statesmanlike action in negotiating a settlement. The twenty-eight year-old Jimmy Hoffa, the story relates, got tired of the "talk, talk, talk" of the DSR strike negotiators and offered the "final compromise."

It was a jurisdictional fight between the AFL and CIO. Feeling was so bitter that Frank Martel, president of the Detroit AFL, refused "even to sit in the same room with those CIO birds." Detroit's Mayor Jefferies had offered a settlement formula—an exclusive contract for the winner of an election and a court test of its validity. The AFL didn't like the idea on grounds that they had a clear majority anyway, so why bother with elections and court tests? They let the Mayor cool his heels in the hallway while they argued about it.

Jimmy, Jay Langley, Victor Tyler, and Leonard Brady of the Teamsters' were there, it was said, principally as a show of force for the AFL. "The Teamsters' Union," the newspaper account stated, "with a reputation for swift and direct action in a labor dispute, was looked upon as the group most likely to meet any CIO attempt to break the strike."

But Jimmy went into action in an unexpected way. "If they were to serve as the fists of the whole Detroit AFL organization, they wanted the issue to be clear-cut and plain," the reporter wrote.

Jimmy was pacing the corridor in shirt sleeves near where the Mayor was waiting for the verdict on his proposal. Suddenly he walked up to the Mayor and said, "Can I see you alone for five minutes, Mayor Jefferies?" "Certainly," the Mayor replied, and together they went into a vacant room and closed the door. Hoffa got right to the point. If the AFL would agree to the election proposed by the Mayor, would he, in turn, agree to drop his demand for a court test? The Mayor would. Hoffa had taken only the five minutes promised.

Now he bounded down the hall to the room where Frank Martel was in conference with the street car men. This was to take hours. "Sometimes Hoffa was with Martel's group and then he would step out and let them talk by themselves for a few minutes. . . . gradually it became apparent that Hoffa was getting somewhere," the newspaper account related, adding, ". . . Hoffa's impatience showed in every gesture and step."

Finally the door opened and the AFL group returned to the meeting room down the hall where the Mayor and his advisors waited. A settlement had been reached. Jimmy's compromise had been accepted. Interviewed by the reporter, he said, "Well, what's the use of just talk, talk, talk? Either settle it or don't settle it. That's the way I look at it."

CHAPTER *6*

Personal and Private

Josephine Poszywak began full time work in a laundry when she was seventeen. The pay was meager and the work, she said, "was the worst kind." It was 1936 and soon the laundry girls were caught up in the strike fever that was sweeping industrial America, especially Detroit. They decided to strike hardly knowing what the word meant. What do you do? Just walk out? Aren't you supposed to talk to the boss first, or at least send him a letter? Suppose he says, you're fired, what then? And what if he hires some goons to shove us around? That's happened, you know. Will anybody help us buy groceries while we're out? Is there some fund or some organization?

The Teamsters' Union responded to their call for help by sending Jimmy Hoffa; twenty-three, experienced, confident, single-minded and tough.

Jimmy organized the women and girls into squads of pickets and started them parading back and forth in front of the laundry, their held-high signs announcing proudly to the world that this particular laundry shop, this tiny dot of floundering human enterprise in the midst of global economic choas, was unfair to its employees.

He took his turn in the circling picket line and as opposite sides of the oval moved counter to each other he looked into the faces of the women, spoke cheerily to them, and lent them his own self-assurance to help overcome their self-consciousness and uncertainty. But it turned out to be one of the few times in his entire career from Kroger's warehouse to the plush office of the General President in Washington, when he did not pay strict attention to the business before him. As he looked into those faces one caught his eyes with such fixed power that it wrenched his head around as they passed. It was, of course, Josephine.

She is a Detroit girl of Polish descent. She is an inch or two shorter than Jimmy's five feet five. In heels she looks nearly level into his eyes. Her once blonde hair is silver gray and stylishly coiffed. Her eyes are sky-blue with a positive sparkle. Her nose is straight and prominent, but not too prominent. She is thin-waisted and well proportioned. She must have been a knockout at seventeen when they first faced each other on the picket line.

But knockout or not she is the only woman ever to attract and hold Jimmy Hoffa's attention. He found little ways to give and get her attention there on the picket line. He would ask her opinion on things, look and speak directly to her when actually addressing several people or the whole group, and ask her to come with him to get doughnuts and coffee for everybody. (It was March and bitter cold.) A couple of days later he asked her to dinner and the movies.

Thus Jimmy Hoffa, not a woman hater but certainly a woman dodger, met his future wife. Like many a man before him generally indifferent to the prospect of matrimony, when the right woman came along he probably never knew what hit him.

They met each other's family, he formallly asked for her hand, and they were married in September at Bowling Green, Ohio. "We got married on Saturday, drove back to Detroit on Sunday, Jimmy went to work Monday morning and I'm still waiting for a honeymoon," is Jo's wifely lament. "I ask him from time to time, why did he ever pick me out? Out of all those other girls at the laundry, some of them a lot prettier than me, why did he pick me? And he always answers, 'You looked like you needed a good meal.' "

They took an apartment and Jo made the easy transition to housekeeping for two. Jimmy was of the old school; no wife of his would hold down a job as long as he was alive and healthy.

A baby girl, Barbara, was born in 1938 and James, Jr. came along three years later. In the meantime they bought a home suitable for raising a family where they live to this day. It is a red brick house in a spacious neighborhood with plenty of green grass and trees. It is not large and it is not fancy, except for a shiny aluminum storm door in front with a scroll grillwork centered with a circled letter "H". It is a big improvement over the houses of his youth, the multi-family dwellings on Toledo and Scotten Streets, the modest bungalows of Brazil, Indiana, and the little shed in Clinton—his mother's house of remorse.

The family of James R. Hoffa can well afford to live in the grand manner. They could have, if they wanted it, a very large house with a library, guests' rooms, maids' rooms, swimming pool—the works. And their reason for not having such a house and living in such a manner has nothing to do with trying to impress the rank and file members of the Teamsters' Union, as has been conjectured. The fact is, it is almost a matter of heredity, bred into the Hoffas. Neither Jimmy's father, grandfather, nor great-grandfather cared much about houses and home-places. They were fundamentally nomads who wanted, when they needed it, a place of warmth and shelter. Aside from that they desired only adequate shelter and safety for their women and children.

Barbara is married now and has a baby and Jim, Jr., is a second-year law student. But they still get a lot of attention from their father and their childhood memories are close:

" . . . We always knew he was somebody special. His name was in the news and people talked. But this didn't affect our home life. He must have been away a lot but we didn't notice; it seems he was always there; and when he was at home he spent a lot of time with us.

"Of course, he had meetings to go to. Sometimes a special Sunday dinner would get cold. We'd wait and wait and finally eat without him. But when he got home Mother didn't fuss, or if she did we never knew about it.

"Everything is stacked against Daddy. Everybody thought he was going to be acquitted. That judge in Chicago practically said so but then something happened. He got the word.

"We loved our house and still do. Daddy told Mother he'd never sell it. It was his first home and he's so proud of it. We share the house. Chucky and Mary Ann O'Brien and their two children live there and all the rest of us, too, whenever we're in Detroit. It gets pretty crowded sometimes. When all of us are there, there aren't enough beds to go around. After supper we talk and watch television for a while and then somebody, about nine o'clock, will yawn and stretch and say, ho-hum, I think I'll go to bed. That starts the rush. Well, the last one to make a move may sleep on the sofa. Maybe even the floor. We call it our Puerto Rican boarding house.

"We used to take a lot of drives on Sundays. Often we went to the Penn-Mar restaurant for lunch or an afternoon snack. And we drove to Port Huron and Mt. Clemens or just out in the country. Did your father take you places? Ours always did.

"He never spanked us. He would laugh at it—whatever Mother scolded or spanked us for. He would say you should spank the child immediately after the incident or not at all. But he disciplined us. Oh! Did he ever! His discipline was trusting in the child and when you did wrong it hurt more than a spanking. Rarely did he holler or get impatient.

"We had a farm and spent weekends and summers there. We learned to drive there. Daddy had a Jeep. He didn't say a word when I knocked over the fence.

"He always wanted to see our grades and if anything didn't please him he'd point that finger . . . He helped with our lessons when we were little kids."

* * * * *

Jimmy Hoffa is the kind of husband who gets the rest of us in trouble. Red roses every anniversary is enough to make the average man choke up on a two-foot putt. Top that with at least one long distance telephone call a day when he is out of town and the society-for-the-protection-of-us-negligent-husbands ought to take action.

His attitude toward his wife is one of attention, affection and protection although he does not shield her from the realities of his public life as some people, including himself, are prone to think. Jo is vivacious and outgoing. She reads and listens and talks. She knows what is going on and she suffers through her husband's troubles as any devoted wife would. But she does not, when he comes home, rush tearfully into his arms and she does not try to make him rehash the days events for her benefit in order to try to keep up with his business affairs as prescribed by the soap operas and ladies' magazines. No wonder he sends her roses.

Josephine Hoffa has been hurt often and deeply. Her husband has been an extraordinarily controversial figure practically all of their married life and only rarely has he been cast in an attractive role in the public press. More times than she can recall journalists or authors have begged interviews on the promise of turning out objective, non-biased accounts only to write stories which in her view were totally biased, totally unobjective and scurrilous. She is understandably reluctant to submit to interviews.

This writer searched the dictionary for words to describe her attitude when he interviewed her and settled on this single one: Wistful. It's meaning, according to Webster's New World Distionary, is: "closely attentive; showing or expressing vague yearnings; longing pensively."

". . . He never did learn how to dance," she said. "I used to imagine I was going to marry a tall, dark and handsome man who was a wonderful dancer. I guess all girls want to be swept around a grand ball room. Oh, well. But when Barbara got marired and Jimmy had to dance the first dance with her, he did it and did a good job, too. Then he danced with me and I asked how in the world he learned to dance and he just said, "Oh, I watch 'em."

"We had no trouble raising the children. We always sat down and explained things to them—like right now with the trial—we don't keep anything from them. Both of our kids are fine but they grow up too fast. He took our boy hunting when he was only seven years old. I told him not to do that, that he was just a baby. He said, "Well, you have to start making a man out of him sometime." They stayed two weeks in northern Michigan. He helped with the children. Barbara had a terrific time with her teething. We took turns every two hours walking her. He was up half the night with her. We spoiled her quite a bit, but she was the first, you know, and it never hurt her. They are not spoiled children.

"I never followed the McClellan Committee hearings. It made me sick—all that stuff I knew wasn't true—and what they insinuated was worse than what they came right out and said. Last Memorial Day Mary Ann made him really laugh by doing some imitations, and I was so glad she did. He hasn't laughed much lately.

"He likes the westerns and he likes music. We watch the eleven o'clock news and then go to bed. He sleeps well. The alarm is set for seven but he's usually up before it rings. He is happier than I am when he gets up. Don't talk to me before I've had my coffee, but he's very cheerful.

"My kids think I sit around in a rocking chair but I'm going to be a modern grandmother. I like being around young people. I'm glad I can do something for the Teamsters'. I'm helping in the political action program, you know. I like to go around and meet the women. They're no better women in the world than Teamsters' wives.

"Jimmy is proud of his family. He's always bragging about how they came over on the Mayflower. . . . We never had any money troubles. Jimmy would say, 'If you can't afford it, don't buy it.' . . . I've tried to make a better dressed man out of him but it's useless.

"When he has to go somewhere I try to put out a shirt, tie and suit for him and usually one of the girls at the office will say, Oh, who dressed him this morning? . . . We have an old fashioned Chirstmas. We like to enjoy our tree a little longer so we put it up a week before Christmas Day and take it down on New Year's Day . . . What was her name? Eileen? Eileen wrote to him once after he was famous. I answered the letter. That's the last we've heard from her. . . . We had a horse at the farm and Jimmy was trying to break him in. He was stubborn and the horse was stubborn, so what happened? The horse fell on him and broke his leg. . . . We used to ride quite a bit when we first got married. . . . I used to bowl a lot when I was a little younger. You pick up jokes at the bowling alley and I brought them home. But Jimmy never told me an off-color joke. In many ways he's very prudish. . . . Never have I heard a bad remark about him."

"Every marriage has its arguments, especially when you first get married. But I figured he argues all day long so why should he have to argue at home. When he opens that front door at the end of the day he's smiling and I'm smiling."

CHAPTER *7*

The Fox
and the
Hounds

Jimmy Hoffa has developed a philosophical attitude about the many investigations and trials that have entertained his enemies for so many years. "I've been investigated on a continuous basis over half my life," he said, "I can look over my shoulder any time and spot somebody shadowing me. They watch me every minute. When I went to Israel to dedicate a hospital they sent them along. They keep my telephone tapped so they can hear everything I say, too. They keep three or four guys busy year-round checking my taxes trying to find a two-bit mistake to pin on me." Who is the mysterious "they"? Pinkerton men hired by employers, Bobby Kennedy's Justice Department boys, Treasury Department agents and Senate Committee investigators.

Is this the voice of a wronged man, or is it whistling past the graveyard? The answer to that question, or at least the answer that will stand up in history, will be decided by the courts. As this is being written Hoffa stands convicted for jury tampering and conspiracy to defraud his own Union, subject to appeals which no doubt will go all the way to the Supreme Court of the United States unless reversed by lower appeals courts.

It is possible to find substance in Hoffa's claim that the Justice Department under Attorney General Robert Kennedy conducted a "vendetta" against him. The McClellan Committee hearings, which focused both light and heat on Hoffa and the Teamsters' Union, were first mentioned by young Kennedy during the 1956 election campaign when he was working in the Democratic camp of Presidential candidate Adlai Stevenson. Just a week before election day Kennedy told reporters that his subcommittee of the Senate Committee on Government Operations would investigate the Teamsters' and Carpenters' unions. Just what these labor organizations had to do with Government operations was not discussed.

Considering the timing of the announcement and the fact that the leaders of these particular unions almost exclusively among national labor leaders were supporting the Republican nominee Dwight D. Eisenhower, the cynical world of presidential politics nodded knowingly. It is doubtful that at this point the presaged investigation was more than a campaign ploy. But ploy or not it soon became a major part of the long-range strategy of the Kennedys in their drive for political power and the greatest prize of them all, the White House.

A few months earlier at the Democratic National Convention in Chicago, Senator John F. Kennedy had come within a handful of delegate votes of winning his party's vice-presidential nomination. Nobody thought he had a chance but his near-miss resulted from surprising support from the Southern so-called conservative wing of the party which, in its well known schizophrenia, hates labor unions per se nearly as much as it loves the pro-labor oriented national Democratic Party. He lost the nomination because the opposite wing of the party went for Senator Estes Kefauver, his opponent in that instance.

The Kennedys were quick to grasp the long-term implications of that situation. Obviously the future demanded two apparently conflicting accomplishments. They had to somehow hold the support of the Southern Democrat Conservatives while winning that of the Northern Liberals. The labor issue was tailor made for such a purpose. Embrace labor; please the North. Attack labor; please the South. On the surface that would seem impossible but to those who knew the labor politics of the time (which continue today) it was fairly easy to do. The Kennedys knew labor politics backwards and forwards. The Teamsters' Union was just as tailor made for the special role it was to play as was the overall issue. Under the leadership of Dave Beck it was nominally Republican and better still, the Teamsters' hierarchy was at odds with that of the now combined AFL-CIO and Walter Reuther, that aging warrior for liberal causes, former firebrand, president of the United Auto Workers and veteran of internecine wars with Jimmy Hoffa's Teamster units in Detroit and vice-president of the AFL-CIO.

"Walter Reuther is one of the most powerful figures in the United States. His influence within the Democratic party is so great that his vetoing of any Presidential hopeful could constitute the kiss of death. Which may explain why the McClellan Committee Under Bobby Kennedy's guidance—concentrated its fire almost entirely on the Teamsters and old-line AFL unions for the "labor mess" while steering its muck raking away from Reuther and the CIO unions. Significantly, most of the labor bosses who came under Bobby Kennedy's withering fire had records of supporting the Republican cause." [1]

The Kennedys picked up Jimmy Hoffa as though he were a touch football and began kicking and passing him around the family circle, thereby playing both sides of the union game. They kept the friendship of Reuther and the liberal Democrats while giving the anti-labor Southerners,

---

[1] "J. F. K. The Man and the Myth," Victor Lasky, MacMillan.

who are forever searching out excuses to tell their constituents to rationalize their professed conservatism with their enduring allegiance to the overwhelming liberal Democratic Party, something to hang their hats on—a reason for supporting them.

In the meantime the Carpenters' Union regained favor with Reuther and the AFL-CIO and was thereby taken off the hook, leaving the Teamsters' alone to face the risk and the wrath of the Committee's investigators. Bobby lit into Dave Beck with all the go-for-jugular zeal for which he is so justly renowned, and soon deposed him. But in Hoffa he had a tough, shrewd and clever adversary, as well as an experienced one. "Some of the employers used to hire private eyes to work me over with a fine-tooth comb," Jimmy says. "Then the Detroit police and politicians got into the act. Later I was the official whipping boy and scapegoat for state politicians. Congress started in on me in 1953 and I thought I was finally getting to the big time."

Fortunately for Jimmy and unfortunately for Bobby the former's experience usually resulted in the latter's failure to trap him or in any way box him in during the Senate hearings. Some of their exchanges were almost funny as Jimmy got Bobby's goat again and again. There was the matter of the Minifons (minature tape recorders):

Hoffa: What did I do with them? Well, what *did* I do with them?

Kennedy: What did you do with them?

Hoffa: I am trying to recall.

Kennedy: You could remember that.

Hoffa: When were they delivered? Do you know? That must have been quite a while.

Kennedy: You know what you did with the Minifons and don't ask me.

Hoffa: What did I do with them?

Kennedy: What did you do with them?

Hoffa: Mr. Kennedy, I brought some Minifons and there is no question about it, but I cannot recall what became of them . . . I have to stand on the answers that I have made in regards to my recollection and I cannot answer unless you give me some recollection, other than I have answered."

In desperation Bobby moved on to another matter which he pursued with similar results. He conducted the hearings like an inexperienced lawyer, which he was. The matter of the Minifons rested along with many other opened but unexplored avenues of the investigation. But unfortunately for Jimmy and fortunately for his antagonists the many charges leveled against him received headline treatment in the nation's press and with so much mud flying some was bound to stick. Whether all, any or none of it was justified is another matter.

In the meantime the Kennedys led public sentiment and other politicians followed it in making Hoffa into the public image of a "bad guy." In the 1958 Congressional elections everybody ran against Hoffa although the Republicans were noticeably less enthusiastic and scattered their fire to cover Reuther, too. The Democrats won in a landslide—their greatest victory since 1932—attesting to the success of the Kennedy's strategy, and guaranteeing its use in their future. From then on in their continuous campaign for the 1960 presidential nomination he was the number one bad example of all that ailed the nation and mankind, ranking in importance with the "missile gap," which, incidently, was closed by a press release thirty days after the new President took office.

The Kennedys promised, singly and as a brother act, to rid the nation of the Hoffa scourge. "An effective Attorney General with the present laws on the books could remove Mr. Hoffa from office," the Presidenttial candidate declared, thus throwing down the gauntlet, thus setting the stage for the establishment of a special "Hoffa unit" in the Justice Department under Attorney General Robert Kennedy, and thus laying the groundwork for Hoffa's claim of a vendetta to "get" him.

CHAPTER 8

Good Guys
and
Bad Guys

True to his campaign promise Bobby Kennedy and a subcommittee of the Senate Committee on Government Operations, chaired by Senator John McClellan (D., Ark.) began investigating the Teamsters' Union in November following Adlai Stevenson's second losing run for the White House. From the very beginning Senator McClellan's chairmanship was in name only. For reasons which have caused much speculation but have never been determined he let Bobby run the show. Some sort of internal argument over jurisdiction between the Labor Committee and the Government Operations Committee resulted in a compromise, special, committee with the governmentese name, "Select Committee on Improper Activities in the Labor and Management Field," with eight members; four from the Labor Committee and four from Government Operations. Senator McClellan was named Chairman and Bobby Kennedy, Chief Counsel.

The facts of life being what they are, Bobby Kennedy no doubt was aware when he initially threatened to investigate the Teamsters' Union that in any organization of comparable size and scope, be it a labor union, big business, or politics, some hanky-panky is bound to be present. He was sure to find something if he looked long enough and hard enough. But it is doubtful that he truly anticipated the hornet's nest he was to uncover. He had no idea Teamsters' president Dave Beck "was corrupt." And he wasn't even thinking of Hoffa. Without them there was plenty to investigate. There was, for example, the case of a union organizer in Los Angeles whose ambition took him to San Diego to attempt to organize juke box operators. He got the word to stay out of San Diego or he would be killed; it was somebody else's territory. He went anyway, was beaten into unconsciousness and awoke with terrible pains in his lower abdomen. He made his way to a hospital, where, Bobby delicately put it, "doctors removed from his backside a large cucumber." He was told if he came back to San Diego again it would be a watermelon.

Obviously such devious matters cried out for Senate investigation and young Kennedy felt deeply that " . . . it is the obligation of people with advantages to lead those who lack them." This fervent sense of *noblesse oblige* led him to delve into the cucumber affair, and other things, on the West Coast early in 1957.

During a momentary lull in investigating activities he telephoned "a friend of a friend" in Seattle apparently just to kill an evening and learned to his amazement from this friend of a friend that Dave Beck was a bad guy, too, "the real evil in the Teamsters' Union." Bobby, who was registered in a Seattle hotel under the name "Rogers" swung into action. His "friend of a friend" whom he called "Mr. X" told him a Chicago labor relations consultant whose real name was Nathan Shefferman had made purchases for Beck which were paid for from the union treasury. Also, the friend of a friend told him, the Teamsters' Union picked up the tab for construction work on the sumptuous Seattle estate of Mr. Beck. With this new evidence the investigation surged ahead.

Bobby, or "Rogers", interviewed a lot of people but couldn't locate the one man he wanted most to see, Frank Brewster, head of the Western Conference of Teamsters, whom he had heard, was a very bad guy, too, and could tell much about Dave Beck if he wanted to. At last, exasperated, he telephoned a Teamster lawyer named Sam Bassett and, presumably using his real name, told him to get hold of Brewster for him or else. Sam arranged a meeting.

Bobby, who doesn't like many people, found Brewster a likeable chap. Brewster was handsome, dressed well and had a small office. Despite these admirable traits, however, Bobby, who inherited a million dollars at twenty-one, was raised in family compounds up and down the east coast, attended private, exclusive schools, traveled abroad in summers and has huge estates in Virginia, Long Island and elsewhere and plush apartments in major cities, felt that Brewster was "living too well." The McClellan Comitee later sustained this evaluation, charging that Brewster did indeed live high on the hog at union expense, with race horses, summer homes, and other niceities usually reserved for "people with advantages."

But the meeting with Brewster produced nothing in the way of information about Beck. Bobby said Brewster became irritated and indignant as the interview progressed. Bobby headed for Chicago.

Genial Nathan Shefferman has made a career out of applying brotherly love to labor-management relations. His letters and sayings and his office walls are cluttered with patriotic and moralistic quotations and his prosaic, personally designed Christmas cards reflect the artist's kindly spirit and warm heart, as well as his shrewd business technique. His sure sense of brotherliness has taken him into the confidence of labor leaders and captains of industry alike, and he loves both sides. His well-known connections on both sides of the bargaining table, however, are not at all improper, for the business of a labor-management consultant is that of a go-between; there's no other way. As a fringe benefit for his union clients he has sometimes assisted them in making purchases of various things at whole-sale prices.

"Have you made any wholesale purchases for Dave Beck?", Bobby slyly inquired. Why yes, he had, although he didn't remember exactly what or how much or how they were paid for. He bought things for many of his friends and clients, why not Mr. Beck? Why, he'd even purchased that famous refrigerator that saved the life of Walter Reuther who was opening its left-handed door for a midnight snack when the would-be assassin triggered a shotgun blast through the kitchen window. "I'll be happy to pick up a few items for you, Mr. Kennedy," the kindly man offered, but Bobby declined politely, finger tips drumming hard on the desk top.

A couple of days later Bobby got a peek at Shefferman's books and learned what he wanted to know about where the money came from that paid for Beck's wholesale purchases. He hustled back to Washington and straight from the airport to the private apartment of Senator John McClellan. (It was during the Christmas holidays and Capitol Hill offices were closed.) McClellan agreed to hold committee hearings on Beck's finances.

Several days later Kennedy had his first face-to-face encounter with Dave Beck when they met in a New York hotel. They had a mild discussion on racketeering in the Teamsters' Union. Beck assured the detective he had nothing to hide, which, by the time he took the witness' chair in front of the committee a few weeks later, was true. By then Bobby knew all he needed to know about the portly labor chief's finances and proceeded to cut him to ribbons with records of his and the union's financial interlocking. The detailed disclosures were sufficient to send the blood pulsing through the veins of the income tax collectors who then descended on Beck like a pack of hungry wolves after a crippled moose. Bobby succeeded in disgracing Dave Beck, causing his resignation as president of the largest union in the world, and sending him to prison. He also paved the way for Jimmy Hoffa's rise to the presidency of the same union, but he hadn't counted on that.

While the Beck affair was taking place Bobby was engaged in countless clandestine activities with spies and counterspies, do-gooders and get-eveners, as well as ambitious and disgruntled Teamsters who hoped to advance through the upheaval that was rocking the great union. The eager eyes and ears of the Kennedy political machine were everywhere and tipsters and con men all over the country seized upon the impending situation for profit. Bobby implied that somebody close to the Teamster hierarchy was feeding him information apparently to hasten Beck's departure. The secondary implication was that whoever was doing it was working for Hoffa. Hoffa, thought by many to be number two man and the logical and likely successor to Beck, stayed in the background. He saw the handwriting on the wall so far as Beck was concerned. "The McClellan Committee was asking for him so I looked for him and found him in the Bahamas," Hoffa said. "I got him on the phone and told him he'd better get on back to Washington but he said his wife wasn't feeling well. I didn't call him again. I knew he was on the run. He kept on running until he ran out of gas. When your nerve runs out, you run, then that hole card don't look so good no more." Hoffa bided his time.

Hoffa said a New York attorney came to him through a mutual acquaintance who recommended him because of his special contacts and knowledge of Senate Committee methods and activities. Kennedy's side of the same story resulted in the indictment and trial of Hoffa on bribery charges.

According to Kennedy's testimony at the trial a graying, dapper, fortyish lawyer named John Cye Cheasty came to see him in his drab Senate office and unravelled a tale of intrigue. Jimmy Hoffa, he said, gave him a thousand dollars to get a job on the Committee staff and there to spy for him. More money was promised if the venture succeeded. Cheasty took the money and rushed to see Bobby and tell all, and he pulled the cash (less expenses) from his pocket to prove his story. Besides, he agreed with Bobby that Jimmy was "an ugly influence." With such high qualifications he was hired on the spot. Bobby said it was clear that here was a man to whom principle meant more than money. (The FBI took the money and set up a twenty-four hour watch over the principal.)

Bobby sent Cheasty back to New York on February 14, 1957 (Jimmy's 44th birthday) with some stale committee documents and instructions to contact Jimmy and tell him he got the committee job and the deal was on. Cheasty gave Jimmy the documents and received from him two thousand dollars which was promptly turned over to the omnipresent FBI. This and subsequent meetings between Jimmy and his newly retained attorney were recorded for posterity by FBI agents using motion picture cameras behind one-way glass windows.

On the evening of the day of the very first picture taking session Jimmy and Bobby had dinner together at the home of a mutual friend, a Washington attorney who urged the two to get acquainted. Their host having passed away, Bobby and Jimmy are the sole survivors of that memorable meeting but following an initial, firm handshake their accounts of what took place reveal little more than their growing hostility toward each other. Naturally Jimmy did not tell Bobby about his agent, and Bobby didn't mention his double agent.

"I can size up a man by his handshake," Jimmy recalls, "This was a guy who thought he was doing me a favor by talking to me." Bobby, no giant himself, was struck by Jimmy's low altitude.

According to Bobby's version Jimmy did a lot of growling about how tough he is. "I do to others what

95

they do to me, only worse," Bobby said Jimmy said. "Maybe I should have worn my bullet-proof vest," Bobby said Bobby said, which would seem to imply that he was going to take a shot at Jimmy.

According to Jimmy, Bobby asked "a lot of personal questions. How I got into the union, how much money I made, and so on. It was like he was asking how a slum kid like me, with no education and no advantages, what right did I have to be a union leader with thousands of members? When he left I said, well, he's a damn spoiled brat."

It was a cold, snowy night and Bobby left the dinner party early for his estate in the Virginia suburbs, warmed by the certain knowledge that soon he would rid society of the undesirable influence of Jimmy Hoffa thanks to his clever maneuver in hiring for the McClellan Committee staff a lawyer already retained by Jimmy. Three weeks later his expectations moved toward fulfillment when the FBI, after watching and taking pictures, arrested Jimmy and found in his possession confidential McClellan Committee documents given him by Cheasty. Bobby was so happy that for once he made an uncalculated, careless statement. If Jimmy wasn't convicted, he said, "I'll jump off the Capitol dome."

Hoffa's lawyer, Edward Bennett Williams, is a real life Perry Mason who practices his profession on behalf of the underdog and rarely loses a case. He believes, and brilliantly asserts his belief, that all men are equal under the law and that no man ought to be thought of as being guilty, especially by the Government or its representatives, until he has exhausted every avenue of legal appeal and proved guilty. Williams is a throwback to earlier generations of Americans when the fires of personal freedom burned with a brighter flame, before the present relatively stratified social structure in which the public press, politicians and opinion leaders automatically and instantaneously judge the accused; suspect or above suspicion; on the basis of social status which is in turn based on a combination of money and accommodation to the status quo.

Edward Bennett Williams gives more than lip service to the principle that a man has a right to defend himself in a court of law regardless of his public image, money, occupation, education or anything. An unpolished labor leader who clawed his way to the top is just as innocent as a silver-spoon-fed society boy unless proved otherwise by due process of law.

In the trial that followed every angle was explored and exploited by the defense. Williams exercised his full prerogatives in examining, challenging and selecting or rejecting jurors. The twelve good men and true finally chosen consisted of eight Negroes and four whites, an unsurprising ratio in the Nation's Capital where the declining white population is sometimes referred to as a colony.

Miss Martha Jefferson, a Negro lady lawyer, came in from Los Angeles to assist defense counsel Williams and this fact was reported in a full-page advertisement in the Washington *Afro-American*. The ad mentioned that Jimmy Hoffa was a proven friend of the Negro race. When Jimmy's old friend from Detroit, ex-boxing champion Joe Louis, dropped by the court room there to greet him warmly in the presence of the jury, much was made of it. As a matter of record Louis and the lady attorney were courting at the time and were later married. He says he came to Washington and to the court house to see her. Courtesy demanded that he say hello to Jimmy Hoffa.

In the real business of the trial Hoffa claimed that he had retained Cheasty on the recommendation of a friend, which is how most attorneys are retained, as an attorney only, and that after that the McClellan Committee hired him. In other words, it was the committee that had bribed Hoffa's lawyer, not the other way around as charged. Jimmy admitted receiving confidential Senate documents from his lawyer, Cheasty. "I didn't think it was ethical to ask about their source," he said. "You don't go around asking lawyers if they are obeying their Bar Association oath. When a lawyer gives you a report or a brief with supporting papers you accept it as privileged information between lawyer and client," he added with considerable logic. "And I never thought to ask him who his other clients were. I've hired a lot of lawyers but I don't think I ever had one who didn't have other clients. I just assumed Cheasty didn't have any conflicting clients and if he wanted to take one he'd drop me. That's what their professional oath calls for. Maybe he thought it was all right to represent me and Bobby Kennedy at the same time. Maybe he should have read his oath and his license."

About this time Bobby Kennedy must have been eyeing the Capitol dome which towers two hundred and eighty seven feet, five and a half inches, above the concrete and is plainly visible from the Federal building on Third Street. On July 19 the jury returned its decision: Not Guilty. "The verdict was greeted with screaming applause by spectators in the jammed courtroom," the *Detroit News* reported.

Jimmy, grinning broadly, turned to receive the tearfully happy embraces of Mrs. Hoffa, Barbara and Jim, Jr.

Edward Bennett Williams thoughtfully offered to send Bobby a parachute.

Bobby looked grim.

CHAPTER 9

Hot Pursuit

Well, they're trying to get you, Jimmy
    Trying to get you, Jimmy
    Jimmy, they're coming after you.
    Every politician and his brother, Too.

Now some folks say he'll go to jail
And others say we'll go his bail
We can't say who's right or wrong
But a million drivers will sing his song.

        "The Ballad of Jimmy Hoffa"
        By Walter M. Breeland

Dave Beck's personal power within the Teamsters' Union was fading rapidly and it was apparent that he would be forced to step down. It was equally apparent that Jimmy Hoffa, far from discredited in the eyes of rank and file Teamsters as a result of his brushes with the law and collisions with the Kennedys, was more popular than ever and more likely than ever to replace Beck as General President of the huge, well-heeled, powerful union. A convention was scheduled for September in Miami where the elections of officers would take place. The sprawling apparatus of anti-Hoffa political and union power moved frantically to prevent the inevitable.

The McClellan Committee in its heyday employed between forty and fifty full-time investigators and had the services, on demand, of hundreds more from the FBI, General Accounting Office, Secret Service and Treasury agents, civil service investigators and post office inspectors. It is impossible to calculate how many man-hours and how much public money was spent at the direction of Bobby Kenendy in trying to bring Hoffa to his knees. Obviously the dollar figure would be in the millions.

The Government investigator used to be a unique type of public servant in our society, rare and respected. Today this is becoming one of the largest categories of Federal employment aside from run-of-the-mill clerks and typists. Virtually every agency, department and bureau has its own staff of "security" personnel whose duties have little or nothing to do with national security in the sense of defending the nation from subversion from within or attack from without. Mainly they are set to watching American private citizens, and each other.

In addition to human investigators the Government employs all the modern electronic and mechanical spys as well. In 1959 the General Services Administration included on its lists of materials available to Federal agencies tape recording equipment that can be concealed under clothing. During one three year period Federal agencies spent $141,136 for Minifons, tiny recording machines, and that is just a brand name for one of many such devices.

The Committee on Government Operations of the House of Representatives reports five thousand telephone taps in Washington alone. The Committee also found that thirty-three out of thirty-seven agencies questioned admitted tapping incoming telephone calls without letting the caller know about it as required by law and common ethics. Even the Federal Communications Commission, which bears the public trust for guarding the public privacy in public communications, permits its employees to monitor incoming calls. A case was uncovered in the

State Department where three employees were tapping the telephones of another employee. It is not at all surprising that many Washingtonians including Government officials, politicians, labor leaders and businessmen conduct their affairs on the assumption that their business and private telephones are tapped and their offices bugged.

More fearsome than the mechanical devices, however, is the new breed of human investigator now infesting the United States Government. He is himself almost a mechanical thing, with machine-like direction and drive, passionately certain of his own infallible morality, and oh so right, so very right, in every blow he strikes. His job, or so its seems, is to find guilty people and then prove it.

This new breed tends to be youngish and slightly built with tousled hair and pink cheeks. He is university educated, wears dark suits with thin lapels, striped ties, black shoes, button-down collars—all very Ivy. He lives in the suburbs with his wife—a female version of himself—and two, three, or more children. His friends are his fellow investigators and they get together at one another's homes on weekend evenings and exchange tales of the evil they encounter and the good they do.

If there is an exception that proves the rules of physical traits outlined above it is in the person of chubby, talkative, cigar-chomping Pierre Salinger; a very un-Ivy young man; who headed a platoon of McClellan Committee investigators that descended on Detroit in August, 1957. This was Bobby's vengeance for the humiliation he suffered upon Hoffa's acquittal in Washington. (His promise to jump from the Capitol dome produced nothing in the way of tangible results aside from amused chatter in Republican circles and at the bar of the National Press Club, much to the chagrin of his more serious enemies.)

Under Bobby's energetic prodding the entire committee staff rededicated itself to the task of nailing Jimmy. In addition to the Detroit contingent, other units fanned out over the nation sifting Teamster financial records and prying into every lead, and sniffing at every trail, however cold.

Miss Lois Long, a clerk in the Clay County Court House at Brazil, Indiana, was surprised one day when she answered an ordinary jingle of the telephone to find it was a long distance call all the way from Washington, D. C. In the excitement she didn't quite catch the caller's name when he identified himself, but he sounded convincingly official. He asked her to please check court records for entries regarding the Hoffa family and he asked her for specific biographical data on the father of James R. Hoffa, Brazil's most famous if sometimes unacknowledged son. She did as requested and was pleasantly surprised some days later to receive a letter of thanks on U. S. Senate stationery signed by Robert F. Kennedy. Bobby was looking everywhere.

In Detroit, the fox's lair, Pierre made contact with the Teamster local unions and with Joint Council 43 of which Hoffa was president. He demanded their books, borrowed a crew of accountants from the Detroit branch of the General Accounting Office and went to work. He had an unproductive interview with Jimmy which is recalled by both, but in separate, mutually unflattering terms. Pierre said the books were purposely in "rotten shape" just to make things difficult for the sleuths. Jimmy said, "See my lawyer."

The Government men methodically ran down everybody the cancelled checks showed as having received money from the Teamsters and questioned them regarding it. At the same time they rooted out potential informers. As Pierre remembered it later when he testified before the committee, Jimmy's business agents wouldn't have much to do with him. He had other problems, too. One prospective witness, he said, skipped the country.

One harassed truck driver was reported by his wife for bringing home a short pay envelope every week because he had to kick-back to a union business agent. Apparently the poor fellow was afraid to make a fuss about it himself. Luckily his wife was made of sterner stuff. Pierre really thought he had something until the driver himself came in. He'd been keeping a mistress on the side and that's where the money went. He brought her with him to prove it. What a fellow tells his wife is his own business.

In Jimmy's personal lock box at the bank they found a deed to some worthless land, some Government savings bonds, an empty paper sack and a rusty paper clip. In the meantime Bobby was haranguing them by telephone from Washington several times daily. Senate committee hearings were scheduled to begin within a few days and the Teamsters convention was drawing near. At last his impatience overcame him and he sent more men to Detroit and went himself.

While ordinary men ordinarily have a few skeletons in their closets, extraordinary men tend to have many. Jimmy had fought his way to the top over the broken and by-passed ambitions of lesser men and some very good men, too, whose only bad luck was in the quality of their competition. Furthermore, most employers react to labor leaders the way dogs react to cats and cheerfully see and tell the worst in them. When under Bobby's feverish pressure Pierre's crew of detectives focused on him it wasn't long until their brief cases fairly bulged with bones to be returned to Washington for a public picking under the batteries of television lights and cameras in the Caucus Room of the Senate Office Building.

Robert Scott once worked for Jimmy as a business agent of a Teamster local in Pontiac, Michigan. They were friends, Scott said, but he broke it off because he got fed up with Jimmy's methods. Under Chief Counsel

Kennedy's careful questioning Scott said a number of very harsh things about his former friend. He said Hoffa had asked him to use his political influence, which he implied was substantial, to get a new trial for a convicted racketeer who was doing twenty to forty in the state pen. He said Jimmy asked him to try to get a liquor license for another unsavory character. And once, Scott testified, Jimmy wanted him to see the Governor on behalf of somebody needing a pardon. Another time he was asked to find a quiet, inconspicuous place to "hide out" Billy Hoffa during a warm spell.

Jimmy replied to these unincriminating but nonetheless character-blackening charges with what Bobby was to call a "classic disavowal": "I am saying that to the best of my recollection I have no disremembrance of discussing with Scott any such questions." Some of the reporters present thought they saw a twinkle in his eye as he delivered that literary pearl. Bobby winced. His finger tips drummed the table.

Robert Scott was an amateur politician on the Democratic side and apparently Jimmy used his contacts. "He wasn't good for nothing else and that's why I had to let him go," Jimmy said, claiming sour grapes. It is not surprising to anybody who knows his dismal record as a political prognosticator that Jimmy would have to find someone else to run his political errands. Had he chosen politics instead of the union for a career he would never have gotten past precinct chairman. He was constantly on the losing side in Michigan politics, a fact well known around Detroit. "His political activities have been equally aggressive but by no means as successful as his union endeavors," wrote Robert Ball in the *Detroit News* in 1953. It's a cinch if he wanted to influence the Governor he had to go through a third party. He certainly had no personal entree having opposed that gentleman with all the vigor he possessed. When he told a politician, as he testified at one point during the McClellan Committee hearings, "he would have political opposition every time he ran for office as far as I was concerned," his threat likely encouraged rather than discouraged its recipient.

The early committee hearings exploited Hoffa's personal financial affairs as much as possible. Bobby and the good Senators openly charged that his frequent cash transactions were grounds for suspicion and that the use of the power and influence of union funds to secure advantages for himself and close associates raised serious moral questions. For his part, Jimmy said, "I reserve the right as an American citizen to believe that the currency of the United States is still solvent and I don't think you'll find anything unusual about cash being used as a medium of exchange in the United States." The Senators were unimpressed.

Guessing at motives is a shaky business, and Jimmy remains close-mouthed about it, but it appears that he protected his personal and family financial interests from public disclosure by claiming large gambling winnings. That is one way of reporting income without revealing its precise source. The Internal Revenue Service doesn't care where you get it as long you pay taxes on it. His income tax returns, which everybody conceded were under constant scrutiny by the authorities, showed about seven thousand five hundred dollars per year income from gambling and "miscellaneous earnings" between 1948 and 1956. It sounded like a lot more when referred to as "over sixty thousand dollars" which is the way Bobby discussed it.

On the other hand it might very well have been gambling winnings. When the Senators and their Chief Counsel sneered at the gambling claim they revealed their ignorance of the Hoffa family background. They have a gambling streak in them as wide as a Freuhauf trailer. Jimmy's Uncle Charlie back in Clay County lived on a rocky, run down farm and gambled for a living. Jimmy's cousin Clyde, who lives in Indianapolis, is thought to make and even take a bet now and then. Jimmy's brother Billy will bet on yesterday's weather if that's the only action in town.

Jimmy did not elaborate on his financial records for the benefit of his tormentors and when they came up with specific cash items broken down from the overall figures of his tax returns or secured elsewhere he generally credited the sums to loans received from friends. It was only when the Senators and Bobby implied or accused him of taking kick-backs from employers that he flared up. "I will tell you that is a lie," he flashed back when Bobby voiced such an insinuation.

His tendency to patience and tolerance throughout this phase of the grilling may have been due to the fact that he'd been through it several times before. Many of the "startling disclosures" were actually old stuff made public as early as 1953 before he was enough of a national figure to attract attention outside of the Detroit area and trade union circles. And all of it had previously been brought to the particular attention of Teamsters' Union members by his enemies both in and out of the union.

The significance of all this was that McClellan Committee press releases had nothing like the anticipated impact. Although the johnny-come-latelies to the world of big unionism, and this included the Senators and the Kennedys, had the idea that rank and file Teamsters would turn on Jimmy, the old timers knew better. Certainly Jimmy knew better. He couldn't wait for the hearings to adjourn to give him more time to campaign for the presidency of the union.

Bobby made no new friends among Hoffa's enemies within the leadership cadre of the Union when he referred

106

to them indirectly as "the dregs of society."[1] Much of the publicity regarding thugs, crooks and ex-cons in the union was over-stated, over-rated and over-exploited but it is true that Jimmy is most vulnerable in the company he keeps, to which he replies that he has no choice but to deal with Teamster officials at every level of the union regardless of his personal opinion of them. The committee built a strong case against him for failing to flush out the ex-cons and racketeers who had infiltrated its ranks but in fairness it ought to be noted that most of them were there before he came along or at least before he became General President.

And Jimmy is quick to point out that they got there before the Landrum-Griffin law was passed in 1959 as the result of McClellan Committee hearings and the work of Senator John F. Kennedy. This law forbids certain classes of convicted lawbreakers from holding union office. "There have been no thugs placed in charge of this union," is his declaration. "There is a Federal law, passed September 14, 1959. That law sets the standards, the caliber of men who can go to work in unions. We are in full compliance with the law."

He couldn't hire an ex-con or a racketeer if he wanted to.

Harold J. Gibbons, 11th Vice President and member of the General Executive Board of the Teamsters' Union, submitted a detailed rebuttal to the committee's detailed accusation:

"It is interesting to see that in three years of investigation in connection with our union, reputed to be completely dominated by racketeers and hoodlums, one hundred and six names were mentioned.

"We searched high and low for sixteen of these names and never found them among our union files or in any

[1] "The Enemy Within," Robert F. Kennedy, Popular Library.

107

respect as being officials or in any way connected with the Teamsters.

"Nine of these names we found to be members of the union who had never held any position other than member. And, you well understand that if an employer hires a person we are obligated under the law to accept him into membership. These were members, but they were heralded as gangsters and hoodlums.

"We found that thirty-four of those mentioned were former officers or employees who were no longer associated with the Teamsters in any capacity.

"We submitted the names of eight others who were officers or employees of the Teamsters who had been arrested but never convicted of a crime.

"We submitted the names of twenty-six people who were officers, agents or employees who were convicted of misdemeanors or felonies before employment by the Teamsters or before election to office. Some of these went back twenty years before the men became active in anything connected with the Teamsters.

"We had thirteen who were convicted while officers or representatives of the union and were still so engaged. Among these thirteen were arrest records consisting of pleas of guilty to city ordinances relating to disorderly conduct or traffic violations, which are neither misdemeanors nor felonies.

"There were some thirteen, as a total, who could be said to be law breakers who were at the time we filed this report still members of the Teamsters and holding office. Out of a membership of more than 1,700,000, that's not a bad record. It seems to me that in a three-year investigation as widespread as it was, that to be able to come up with only thirteen violators was a case of the mountain having labored and brought forth a mouse."

Jimmy got in the last word:

"I wonder if you could take a million and seven hundred thousand Democrat and Republican party members and workers, and take the elected officers out of that group, the local city chairmen, county chairmen, committeemen and state chairmen, and come up with a record as clean as ours? I doubt it. Or take that many small businessmen or big businessmen, or school teachers or any group. I'll compare Teamsters man for man."

Before the Landrum-Griffin law was passed requiring rigid financial reports by unions, immunity to financial reporting was the big attraction to potential crooks. A businessman or a bank clerk with larceny on his mind is somewhat deterred by ordinary business or bank audits and, ultimately, the Internal Revenue Service which is always poking into their books. Since enactment of the financial reporting requirements it is doubtful that labor unions are any more attractive to racketeers than any other money-handling enterprise.

A single footnote seems necessary. Some of the "charges" against union business agents and officers aired by Bobby and his moralistic investigators were so petty they were silly, tending to sustain the idea that they were bent on "getting" Jimmy and the Teamsters.

One, for instance, had to do with the solicitation of employers to buy tickets to a Teamster-sponsored dinner. This, of course, is common practice among civic groups, church groups, the political parties—virtually any fundraising endeavor. But Bobby construed this to be an attempted "shake down" of employers. In a related charge a Teamster was accused of perjury because he denied asking his boss to buy a hundred dollar dinner ticket. Another indictment accused a Teamster official of charging a private long distance telephone call to his union credit card and putting an airline ticket for his wife on his union expense account. While these are unethical things to do, they aren't exactly unknown in our expense account, credit card conscious society, and hardly seem worthy of the attention of Bobby and his dragon slayers.

A number of the published accusations were bribery charges against Teamster business agents and officers who supposedly took money from employers to pay for "sweetheart" contracts and other favors. But, strangely, the corresponding employers were not charged. Bribery is a two-way street. The *New York Times* asked why the employers were not prosecuted along with the union men. "If there were illegal payments, the illegality was as much on the part of those who made them as those who received them."

Jimmy came out of the first McClellan Committee hearings, not smelling like the proverbial rose, but undamaged to any discernable extent in the eyes of rank and file Teamsters, either, and the latter was the important thing to him. Bobby, on the other hand, showed need of seasoning. It was common knowledge in Washington at the time that Attorney General William P. Rogers found Bobby's work so amateurish as to preclude court action.[1] He was ill-prepared when he got Jimmy in the witness chair and unprepared to follow through on matters he himself had brought up.

But maybe Jimmy had the advantage right from the start: "I sat down and put on paper everything I could think of they might ask questions about. Then I got with the lawyers and went over every item. We'd rehearse what we thought Kennedy would do and we got it right damn near every time. He's not the brightest fellow in the world, you know. And he had to investigate for weeks to find out what we already knew. It's a terrible strain

---

[1] "The Pursuit of Hoffa," Sidney Lens, *The Progressive,* Feb., 1963.

to go before that committee day after day, but when you don't have anything to hide it don't bother you. I know what I done wrong and what I didn't. I know what they'll uncover and what they won't. That's two thirds of the worrying. All my life I've been under investigation."

CHAPTER *10*

The
Top Rung

Immediately after his acquittal on the bribery charge in the Cheasty case Jimmy plunged into the race for the presidency of the Teamsters' Union. He called a meeting of his supporters in Chicago and they roared approval of his candidacy and his program. He presented a nine-point platform—one of the few times he expressed his union philosophy and goals in writing.

He promised greater utilization of the vast resources of the International to finance organizing and collective bargaining activities by lower level units of the union. "The International is not a banking institution," he said in an oblique reference to Beck's obsessive attention to income, investments and the balance sheet. He urged his friends to support his oft-stated aims toward area-wide contracts with employers. He said he would expand the International's research facilities for the benefit of and use by lower echelon units. He pledged cooperation with the AFL-CIO and other unions "provided there is recognition of our jurisdiction and reciprocity of cooperation." He endorsed the labor code of ethics drawn up by the AFL-CIO spelling out rules for democratic processes within unions, safeguarding health and welfare funds, conflicts of interest, racketeering and other local union matters, but he specifically refused to okay the prohibition of pleading the Fifth Amendment, citing a Supreme Court opinion that use of the privilege cannot justify an attempt to "discredit or convict a person who asserts it."

Jimmy has never "taken the fifth" (preferring to rely on his convenient "forgettery," according to Senator Karl Mundt, a member of the McClellan Committee) but some of the other Teamsters who appeared before the committee did many times. Bobby dismissed Jimmy's testimony as "a curious and practically unfathomable mixture of ambiguity, verbosity, audacity and mendacity" and expressed the view that Hoffa, while refraining from personally using the sanctuary offered by the Fifth Amendment, encouraged others to do so as a means of preventing them from incriminating him. There are others who think his baffling syntax was deliberate, and successful. Certainly he cannot be faulted for exercising extreme caution in recalling details of events long past. "All they need is two persons who say you're a liar and you're on trial for perjury," he once explained, "and how often can you be lucky?"

Jimmy threw himself into the business of getting elected to the highest office in his union. The McClellan Committee hearings were a nuisance but he had learned long ago to husband his energy night and day in order to continue working night and day. The insults handed him by Bobby and the Senators were but slight pinpricks on his thick exterior. There were times when his eyes dulled and drooped and his shoulders slumped in his chair. If, on these occasions, his enemies thought he was weakening they were very mistaken. He was merely withdrawn from the proceedings, thinking his own thoughts about things he considered more pressing or more important, or resting.

Bobby threw himself and his entire staff into the continuing business of investigating Jimmy, beginning the day after the first series of hearings adjourned. It was August 24, 1957 and the Teamsters convention was set to begin September 30. "Some people thought we shouldn't have hearings just before the Teamsters convention," Bobby said earnestly, "But if we didn't make public the evidence until after the convention the delegates would always say, 'God, if we'd known all that, we'd never have voted for him!' " Plainly he felt it his solemn duty to use his advantages to expose Jimmy in time to cause a revolted Teamster membership to reject his bid for the General Presidency. News awaited him.

When the Senate hearings opened on September 24, Jimmy was in Miami preparing for the forthcoming convention that meant so much to him. This didn't prevent Bobby from assailing him for all he was worth. The hearings went on from early in the morning until, sometimes, as late as nine-thirty at night. As a normal thing, Senate committee meetings meet from ten a.m. until twelve noon. Bobby hurried along while the Senators, when they were in attendance which wasn't much of the time, sat quietly. "I don't want to go into all those details," he impatiently admonished a friendly witness whose testimony was too slow to please him.

On Tuesday committee chairman McClellan announced his intention to call Hoffa to the stand again on Saturday. On Wednesday a New York grand jury indicted him for perjury in connection with an old wire tapping charge. Hoffa's lawyers appealed to Senator McClellan who agreed to wait until after the convention but in the meantime issued another public relations blast aimed at destroying Hoffa's chances of election. The perjury indictment was later dismissed by the Supreme Court.

The committee issued an interim report listing some thirty-three "improper activities" which had the effect of accusing Hoffa of being unfit and unworthy of any position of trust in the labor movement. In addition, Senator McClellan, or Bobby over his signature, more likely, wired Teamster leaders gathered in Miami that many of the delegates likewise assembled there might have been elected or chosen illegally.

Pressure came from every direction. Thinking they had Jimmy down, they piled on like little boys in a school yard. Secretary of Labor James P. Mitchell issued a warning to the delegates to weigh carefully the charges against Hoffa. Thirteen rank and file Teamster members went into court in Washington claiming convention delegates had been improperly selected and got a temporary injunction against the election.

Jimmy sent his lawyers into the breach and the next day the order was set aside. The disgruntled members took their case to the Supreme Court but Chief Justice Earl Warren refused to reinstate the injunction. The election was on.

These events served to solidify Jimmy's support rather than destroy it as it was intended to do and hoped for by his enemies. He was not a shoo-in. Had the outsiders stayed out of it, it is barely possible that his opponents might have mounted a successful coalition against him. But with so much unsolicited advice the Teamsters' reaction was like a teen-age love affair. Try to break them up and they run off and get married.

Several able and powerful Teamsters coveted the top spot and vigorously pursued it. Thomas L. Hickey and William Lee, both vice presidents and well-known in the union, were off and running. U. S. Representative John P. Shelley of San Francisco, a Teamster member and former official, filed his name with the nominating committee. Thomas J. Haggerty sought the first prize, too. Hoffa won with a rousing seventy-two percent of the vote—1,226. Lee received 314 and Haggerty got 143. The other candidates dropped out in pre-election maneuvering.

Jimmy did some wheeling and dealing in the manner of traditional "smoke-filled-room" politics to win his big majority. As indicated, he exploited the opposition of

Washington politicians and other outsiders to the fullest. More importantly, however, he patched up old differences with the West Coast group which had been more or less anti-Hoffa oriented. Einar Mohn, formerly Beck's number one aide and a rising star in his own right, was named Chairman of the Western Conference of Teamsters. Joseph J. Diviny, a card carrying Teamster since 1923 and a vice president since 1952, was appointed to membership on the General Executive Board along with George E. Mock, an experienced and expert organizer who held the position of International Organizer—a very respected place in trade union hierachy. All were Californians and all were "good guys" so far as the McClellan Committee's press releases were concerned, although there is no reason to think the latter had anything to do with their advancement by Hoffa. It was pure politics, which is not to say they weren't capable and deserving.

An analysis of the vote at the Teamsters' 1957 convention by D. W. Salmon, research director of the Western Conference of Teamsters, attributed 189 of the 477 votes against Hoffa to "reform" motives. Bobby can take credit for these. The remaining, bulk of the anti-Hoffa ballots were cast by personal followers of his opponents.

The tone of the convention was described by John English, secretary-treasurer and grand old man of the union, who, during the proceedings said:

"We are here today at the most crucial time in the history of the Teamsters' Union. We are being watched by everybody all over the country. Yes, they have people here to our left and right from the FBI, the Senate Rackets Committee and probably the AFL-CIO watching what we do.

"I am standing here telling you that we are going to place in nomination the name of James R. Hoffa, the champion of the Teamsters' movement. . . . We don't care what other people think, we are nominating

Hoffa for what he has done for the organization. . . .
There may be a little trouble going on here and there,
but he will take care of that."

When the roll call vote passed the point at which
Hoffa's election was a certainty the huge convention
crowd grew restive. When it was finally over pandemo-
nium broke loose in the hall. He stood up to the tremendous ovation and beckoned his wife to his side.
He embraced her and kissed her and together they waved
back to the cheering delegates. Jimmy mounted the po-
dium to deliver his acceptance speech. He was, at forty-
four, leader of the world's largest, richest, most powerful
union, presiding over more than a million and a half
dues-paying members and with a thumb on the most
strategic industry in the land. At that moment he felt
the full weight of the responsibility. His emotion-packed
speech was perhaps the most candid and revealing of
his entire career and for that reason it is printed here
in its entirety:

I want to say humbly and with the deepest sense of
gratitude, thank you for this great honor which you have
granted me. I realize all of the pressure that has been
placed upon you and this great international union.

I appreciate deeply this vote of confidence. I want
to promise you here and now I will devote myself and all
my energies to serve you honestly and sincerely. And with
God's help, I pledge to do all in my power to lead you
and this organization to a position of respect and honor
in the eyes of the rank and file of labor; in the eyes of
the nation; in the eyes of the world.

I am your servant by virtue of my office as general
president. This international exists for you and for the
membership, however large or small the local union might
be. We are teamsters together, and I pledge to you that
your problem is my problem.

The resources of this great international union will be spent for the benefit of the membership in the never-ending fight for justice and dignity for the workers we represent.

I pledge to you that this union will be a model of trade unionism. I need time and I need the support of each and every one of you to accomplish this task. And I say to you, the rank and file, our million and a half members, I want to hear from you, I want your advice, I want your guidance, I want your help.

If you are dissatisfied with anything that is being done, or in the way this union is being run, I want to hear from you. I believe in good, honest trade unionism. I believe in the welfare of our members. This union will practice democracy in its fullest form, notwithstanding our enemies.

To say that I do not feel deeply about the charges that have been made against me would be untrue. To say that it has not been tough would be untrue. I am a family man. I have a wife and children. I am proud of my family. They know how I believe in the cause of labor. They know this is my life's work and I am not ashamed to face them at any time for anything I have ever done. I will fight to defend myself and to keep the name of Jimmy Hoffa as a symbol of good trade unionism and as a symbol of devotion to the cause of labor. Let's go back and look at what happened to the labor movement in this country in the last fifty years. At the beginning of that period the word 'labor' was something that people hated. Slave wages and slave conditions existed. We know that men like Samuel Gompers, Dan Tobin, William Green, Phil Murray and others were smeared. They were ridiculed. They were investigated and persecuted. Yet they kept fighting. Were they destroyed? No. Did they stop? No. And each hour, each day, they kept plugging away to the point where labor is and was recognized as a vital and important force in the American way of life. You know my background; you know my experience. I have given twenty-five years of my life fighting for this union. I have fought for what I believe is right and good against forces more vicious than you can ever imagine. I propose to continue that fight as long as I live.

Labor has made a greater contribution to the growth of this country than any other single force. We have fought for free public schools; the right to vote; to put an end to debtor's prison; for child labor laws. We have fought for minimum wage laws, for the eight hour day, for Social Security, for the fundamental right of workers to organize. Yes, we have fought for human rights and for the dignity and freedom of the American worker.

Yet today labor is under attack. This international union has just come through the most vicious attack any group of workers has ever experienced. From every side, inside and outside the labor movement, we have been subjected to accusations and charges of every sort and description. Never in history has so much outside effort been exerted on the internal affairs of a free organization.

I have no fight with the McClellan Committee, nor have any desire to obstruct a true and honest investigation. Investigations by committees of Congress to aid in legislation have a useful and proper place in America. But when a Congressional committee concentrates on a personal attack or misuses its power, it can be dangerous for all of us. Something is wrong when a man may be judged guilty in a court of public opinion because some enemy or some ambitious person accuses him of wrongdoing by hearsay or inference. What is happening to our historic principle that a man is innocent until proven guilty?

Something is wrong when newspaper headlines have more force than a court of law, or a jury of one's fellowmen. Something is wrong when some Americans begin to find fault with the Bill of Rights for which our people have died.

The law should not be a weapon of politics. We are taught that our law is the backbone of our democracy. Let's not write law on the front pages of our newspapers. Let us keep law in the statute books and in the courts of justice.

Destruction of the basic priciples of due process and the use of the lawmaking function to smear a man's reputation without the protection of judicial processes is one of the greatest threats to freedom and the rights of the individual that America has faced in our lifetime. I want to say that a great injustice has been done to the individual members of the Teamsters' Union. You are the people whose good name has been smeared.

And I want to say this to the whole country: the working American men and women who make up this International Brotherhood of Teamsters are your next-door neighbors. They aren't gangsters. They aren't hoodlums. They are respected citizens who live next door to you; who go to the same churches and synagogues; whose children go to the same schools that your children go to; who serve the Red Cross and the Community Chest the same as you do. Our members belong to the same clubs and societies as you. These people are Americans. I'm proud to be one of these people.

Something has happened to the labor movement in recent days. I am ashamed of what I see within labor's ranks. I see men who would betray principle to get a better headline. Samuel Gompers did not formulate his program by reading the morning newspapers.

I have said before and I repeat now that we will never leave the AFL-CIO voluntarily. We dispute the charges that have been leveled against us. It is unfortunate that the AFL-CIO accepted unproven charges without full investigation as to their merits. We condemn the hasty action taken with regard to our international union. We condemn the effort to interfere with our internal affairs. We believe in the autonomy of international unions and shall defend our autonomy as teamsters.

We have taken action at this convention to comply fully and properly with proper ethical demands of the AFL-CIO. We have repeatedly stated that this action would be taken at our convention. The Teamsters' Union will never fire the first shot in a civil war in the American labor movement. I have worked long years and I have fought hard in the cause of America's workers. I believe strongly in unity and cooperation. Only anti-labor forces will profit from a split in the house of labor.

We have no desire to become a party to disorganizing the organized. There is too much to do—too many workers who need to be organized, too many workers who need better conditions—to waste our energies on internal warfare. I say that it would be a tragedy if the selfish action of a few ambitious men in the top leadership were permitted to destroy the hard-won unity of the American labor movement.

We will do everything in our power to remain within the united labor movement. The Teamsters' Union has every hope and intention of giving full cooperation in the fight for economic justice. I hope that the hasty threats of expulsion will be withdrawn as time and what we do to prove our sincerity and that we are decent trade unionists and useful citizens.

But I say to you that if certain forces succeed in driving us from the united labor movement for their own selfish ends, let me give them this warning. Separation didn't hurt the machinists. It didn't hurt the carpenters. It didn't hurt the mine workers. And it won't destroy us. The Teamsters' Union will continue to live and grow.

If these people succeed in forcing the teamsters out of the federation, and attempt to raid our organization, mark my words and mark them well, we will be ready to defend ourselves with every ounce of strength we possess.

Again I say I hope that we will not be deprived of the opportunity to serve the united labor movement. We have work to do—all of labor together—and we are prepared to cooperate with all the resources at our command.

Some so-called labor leaders have fallen into a trap. They fear anti-labor legislation, and rightly so. In their fear, they have been misled by bad advice to condemn so-called labor corruption more often than the union haters. It would seem to me that the leaders of organized labor should be emphasizing the good things in the labor movement. Instead, they wind up cooperating with labor's enemies. They forget that tomorrow it will be their turn to face the enemy. I hope they are able to fight back.

Instead of concentrating on the protection of individual rights and human freedom, they keep quiet because they are afraid. This is not leadership. This is surrender, and that is something we will never do.

It is easy to accuse a man of corruption. It is too bad that some people are always willing to believe the worst. Too bad that some leaders of labor ignore fair play and truth and join the yapping of the union haters. I say to you that we face the serious situation of bitter anti-union legislation unless the labor movement begins to fight for due process and an end to unproved accusations. If we become too timid to fight for what is right and just, we will lose in the legislatures what we have won on the picket lines.

As has been said on many occasions by such leaders as John L. Lewis, there is more than enough legislation on the local, state and Federal books to handle and prevent whatever corruption there may be within the ranks of labor.

There has been a concentrated effort to bring disunity and confusion upon us. We cannot ignore the fact that certain outside pressures want to dominate or destroy this union. We teamsters have not lost our unity, and we shall not lose it.

I have spent twenty-five years of my life in the labor movement. I have fought the opposing forces with every device at my command. I have been beaten, threatened, abused and smeared. But I will continue to fight. I'll fight with every weapon at my command to protect our union's unity and strength. We shall go forward. We are teamsters. We are brother unionists. As brothers, we may fight among ourselves. But we shall present a united front against any attack from the outside and we shall never surrender our birthright—to fight against all odds in the service of our brotherhood.

Among all the charges, no one said we have failed to organize. No one has said we have failed to bring to our membership a program of wage gains and improved security never equaled in the history of organized labor. We have done these things because we have worked together in the service of our rank and file membership.

Let no outsiders weaken us by destroying that unity. Let no outsiders by propaganda weaken the confidence of our rank and file membership. Let us bury our differences; let us work together as a team; let us stand united; let us serve the interests and protect the welfare of our membership every hour of every day. By closing ranks, by settling our differences peacefully and democratically within our own house, we can move forward to build a greater and stronger Teamsters' International Union."

When he sat down amid the tumultuous demonstration it is doubtful that any delegate, not even those who had voted against him half an hour earlier, regretted the choice of the convention. He was talking Teamster language, which is pure Hoffaese.

Bobby said the convention was rigged from start to finish. Senator McClellan, the Secretary of Labor, editorial writers, news commentators and hundreds of political speech-makers joined in the denunciation. Thus encouraged the "dissident thirteen" who had tried to prevent Hoffa's election by court order renewed their legal attack. After twenty-two days of legal wrangling in court the defendants (Hoffa and other newly elected officers) agreed voluntarily to a settlement providing for a board of monitors to oversee Teamster activities. Regardless of the wisdom of this particular decision, it serves to illustrate a key Hoffa characteristic; his willingness to trade current expediencies for tomorrow's headaches.

Other anti-Hoffa forces at work during this period aimed toward the AFL-CIO convention scheduled for December 5th at Atlantic City. The main business of this frosty affair was to be action against the Teamsters' Union for its alleged corruption and the misconduct of its elected leaders. George Meany, the president of the AFL-CIO, had sounded the theme by pronouncing Beck unfit for union office. On September 5th the Ethical Practices Committee had met and heard Beck, Hoffa and others state their cases for themselves. Hoffa made an impassioned plea, explaining in more temperate tone and in more detail than ever before or since his personal financial affairs and his associations with ugly characters within and outside the union. The committee summarily rejected his testimony. On September 16th it submitted its report to the AFL-CIO's Executive Council saying Hoffa had used union funds for personal advantages and consorted with various racketeers and permitted them to hold places of influence within the union. This report was ordered (by the AFL-CIO Executive Council) read at the Teamster convention and placed in its permanent record.

After considerable debate and in an angry, resentful atmosphere the Teamsters' Executive Board decided to read the complete report to the convention and this was done. At this point the majority of the Board was eating out of Hoffa's hand; the decision could not have been made without his acquiescence. In what was undisputably a spontaneous surge of anger and defiance the delegates noisily moved, seconded and struck the report from the convention minutes. Thereafter there were no illusions among Teamster officers regarding the upcoming AFL-CIO's conclave in Atlantic City. When they finally arrived, the Teamster delegation found the air inside Convention Hall colder than the icy, wind-swept Boardwalk outside.

The only thing they had going for them was sheer size and money. They were, with more than a million and a half members, the largest AFL-CIO affiliate and contributed $800,000 per year to its treasury. But this time there was no relenting. The Teamsters were unceremoniously kicked out of the house of labor, but not until after venerable John English had gotten in a few memorable words:

"We ask for one year, after giving you fifty years. We ask for one year to clean up our house. Beck is gone. Brewster is gone. And Brennan is gone. There is only one man—Jimmy Hoffa. And Jimmy Hoffa has done more for our International Union than anybody connected with it, including myself. How in the hell can we kick him out? . . . I am coming near the end of my days. . . . The Teamsters will get along. We won't forget our friends. . . . As far as our enemies are concerned they can go straight to hell."

Meany, Reuther and the others looked away as the old gentleman had his say. Then the Teamster delegation arose and walked silently from the hall.

"A lot of people in the AFL-CIO were very scared when the investigation came along," commented Harold Gibbons, "The expulsion was largely a case of throwing Teamsters to the dogs in the hope that they might avoid further heat themselves."

Jimmy was never as cocky about being thrown out of the AFL-CIO as about other setbacks. It is perhaps the one thing resulting from the McClellan Committee action that he regrets most. He made it plain from the beginning that he was ready to turn the other cheek to insults hurled his way by Meany and Reuther and other big-wigs of the Federation. Following expulsion he was careful not to burn any bridges that remained.

Hoffa, through the years since 1957, has made many overtures aimed toward healing old wounds and eventual re-affiliation. He's even said nice things about his old Detroit rival, Walter Reuther. Once he publicly conceded that Reuther was the logical successor to Meany as president of the merged labor group. He said, "You gotta give the devil his due." But Meany has been curt and unreceptive and Reuther has shown no enthusiasm. It is not likely that a reunion will come about during the old plumber's tenure. It remains to be seen how Reuther will act when he is on his own.

Jimmy was busy throughout the balance of the year following his election cleaning up the debris left in the aftermath of all the efforts to "get" him. His New York trial on a wiretap charge ended in a hung jury. Later, after a second trial, he was acquitted. The perjury rap hastily hung on him during the hectic convention week, it has been noted, was dismissed by the Supreme Court. Wiretap evidence, or rather evidence obtained by wiretapping, could not be used in a Federal court, it was ruled. The Federal Government was trying to use wiretapped evidence to convict Jimmy of wiretapping.

The McClellan Committee had an interesting double standard regarding wiretapping. While making pious noises about alleged tapping by "bad guys" it cheerfully played back its own tape recordings to condemn them. Further, it was common knowledge among Senate staff personnel that Bobby had as a permanent staff member one Edward ("Second-Story") Jones, a gentleman of vast experience with electronic listening devices, wiretapping and bugging instruments, and not known to have any other merchandisable talents. A penetrating comment was made by Edward Bennett Williams: "You can't tap wires with one hand and prosecute wiretappers with the other."

There was a brief encounter between Jimmy and Bobby at the court house during one of his New York trials. As usual, their separate versions of it vary somewhat.

The meeting didn't make much of an impression on Jimmy who remembers only that it was in an elevator and that he said: "Hello, Bobby. How are you getting along?" And that Bobby, "Gave me that silly smile and went on about his business."

Bobby's account has more detail: "I asked him how it felt to be president of the Teamsters' Union, a post to which he had been elected about two months after his bribery trial. He replied, 'Greatest job in the world, but it's keeping me busy.'

"Then I inquired how his wiretap was going. He gave me rather an interesting answer to that. 'You never can tell about a jury,' he said. 'Like shooting fish in a barrel.' Outside on the court steps we parted. 'Take care,' he said."

CHAPTER 11

Running the Teamsters' Union

While Bobby and his staff on the U. S. Senate payroll doggedly prepared further activities in pursuit of Jimmy, the dowdy labor chief turned to his first responsibility; running the giant union. With all the publicity focused on his extra curricula affairs the casual observer is prone to forget, if indeed he was ever aware, that the main business of the union, organizing new members and negotiating labor-management agreements, went on despite headlines, hearings, or anything. Jimmy never neglected these matters—the real innards of union management—and the proof lies not only in knowledge of his methods and intensity of personal effort but also in results. During this period, 1958-60, the Teamsters' Union grew steadily while other unions lost steadily. These included smug Walter Reuther's automobile workers, pompous Dave McDonald's steel workers, and fidgity Jim Carey's electricians. (Of the three only Reuther remains in power today.) More importantly to the rank and file member who faces his wife every Friday over a pay envelope, Teamsters' wages continued to grow bigger and faster than those of all other industries. Wages for over-the-road drivers hit three dollars per hour and "conditions" bettered as Jimmy adroitly maneuvered employers as well as recalcitrant local union overlords into area-wide labor contracts and worked toward his dream of a nation-wide agreement.

These achievements were accomplished under the watchful gaze of the court appointed Board of Monitors, originally conceived and accepted by the General Executive Board to satisfy the enduring suspicions of a small group of rank and file members who came to the surface just in time to try to upset Jimmy's election in 1957. "We accepted the monitorship in lieu of a long drawn out court case," Jimmy said. "At that time, however, it was understood that it would be just for one year and we would have another convention in January, 1959. But the monitors perpetuated themselves in office."

Under the terms of the court order the plaintiffs were to nominate one of the monitors. Their choice was Godfrey P. Schmidt, the New York labor-relations lawyer who had taken their case to court for them originally. Another member of the Board, and its Chairman, was nominated by the plaintiffs and the defendants jointly. He was Martin F. O'Donoghue, a Washington, D. C., lawyer-politician who had represented the Teamsters' Union at various times past. The third member, nominated by the defending Teamsters' International, was attorney Daniel B. Maher.

The relationship between the Board and the Union in the beginning was one of constructive cooperation. Hoffa and his lieutenants met often with O'Donoghue, Schmidt and Maher to review the monitors' findings and recommendations and to make corrections where possible. Jimmy chose to ignore the derogatory news stories that began appearing with increasing regularity although they had all the earmarks of being monitor-inspired and in some cases openly quoted monitor sources. The Consent Decree had made no provision for a public relations program on the part of the Board. But Jimmy determined the best strategy was to ride with the punches until the year was up, a new convention held, and the Board of Monitors dissolved.

In due time the General Executive Board scheduled the convention for March, 1959, carefully stretching the period of monitor oversight to approximately sixty days beyond a calendar year's end from its inception. But then, to the surprise of the Teamsters and many outside observers, Godfrey Schmidt petitioned the court to extend the period on grounds that a fair convention was impossible until such time as the Union was purged of undesirable elements, meaning Hoffa. Judge Letts upheld Schmidt's point of view and the convention was summarily and indefinitely postponed.

Hoffa's view that the Board of Monitors sought to "perpetuate itself" was upheld by a number of non-Teamster on-lookers. For example, Professor William Goffen, who teaches law at the College of the City of New York, wrote in *The Nation* in April, 1960:

"Schmidt's opposition to a new ballot (which under the terms of the agreement would have dissolved the monitorship and terminated the lawsuit) is understandable for reasons other than his professed concern for the welfare of the rank and file Teamsters he represented. Since February, 1958 the Board of Monitors has taken more than $350,000 in fees out of the dues of rank and file membership. In addition, Schmidt and his co-counsel have so far claimed sums amounting to $210,000, plus expenditures exceeding $17,000 for services as plaintiff's attorneys."

At this point Jimmy Hoffa just about had his belly full of the Board of Monitors. The Teamsters' Union swung into action in a massive effort to end the Consent Decree, terminate the Board and call a new convention.

In several legal moves they gave evidence to a Court of Appeals showing that Board Chairman Martin O'Donoghue, who was supposed to be impartial, had actually vowed to cleanse the labor movement of Jimmy Hoffa and further, was using against Jimmy information gleaned from Teamster files when he represented the Union. In the face of this proven conflict of interest, O'Donoghue resigned. Next Jimmy's lawyers submitted data proving that Godfrey Schmidt also was involved in conflict of interest affairs. The Court of Appeals, agreeing with the Teamsters, found that while serving as a monitor representing Teamster members the labor relations attorney was also representing several employers in their negotiations with the Union. Schmidt was dismissed from the Board.

Meantime another arm of Jimmy's staff operation was at work. For a man unrenowned for his ability to select subordinates and delegate authority, Jimmy landed a gem of a man in Sidney Zagri, his Legislative Counsel. Smooth, tough, Harvard-trained Zagri is as brainy as he is energetic and the latter characteristic in him is phenomenal.

Zagri drives himself as well and as hard as he drives his secretaries and staff assistants. He absorbs research material by the reams and turns out reports and related matter in like quantity, while taking scores of telephone calls, making others, and keeping appointments in his own office and on Capitol Hill. He is the kind of man you want working for you, but you'd be a fool to work for him.

Zagri is big and fleshy and as strong as a tractor-trailer rig but his manner is gentle and his tongue is velvet when he is engaged in the ancient and honorable art of lobbying. His multifarious activities seldom appear above the surface but his bubbles are everywhere, if you know what to look for. He has learned well one of the first lessons of lobbying in Congress—they play the star system and the Senator or Representative you are dealing with is the star, to be glorified, admired, coerced and persuaded, but never outshown. A good lobbyist is nearly invisible in official Washington.

Zagri's handling of the matter of the Board of Monitors was a masterpiece in lobbying. On April 13, 1960, four United States Senators; two Republican conservatives and two Democratic liberals; took the Floor of the Senate to enter impassioned pleas for justice for, of all people, Jimmy Hoffa.

On the very same day on the opposite side of the Hill eleven Members of the House of Representatives spent two hours similarly engaged in one-sided debate.

The question posed by the august lawmakers was this: If the Landrum Griffin law passed in September, 1959 was sound in its provisions for protecting the rank and file union members from undemocratic practices in the selection of their leaders, why can't the Teamsters' Union have a convention and hold its election under that law's provisos?

Senator Homer Capehart of Indiana, the epitome of a conservative Republican whose rags to riches personal story seemed to enrage the Kennedys who often used him in illustrations of the typical bad example of a conservative Republican, led off: He said the newest labor law was passed "to make certain that the rank and file of union members had a right to elect their own officers in free and open elections." He said he had been informed by Teamster members that "as a result of the monitoring system in effect at the present time, these people are denied an election."

The late Senator Styles Bridges of New Hampshire, the senior Republican and his party's wheelhorse in the Senate, said: "I am one of the many Senators who have been receiving communications relative to this situation. They are disturbing. We had hoped the monitors appointed by the Federal court would help to clear up the situation."

Senators John Carroll of Colorado and Wayne Morse of Oregon joined their Republican colleagues:

"The courts should not under the broad power of equity be interfering with 1,600,000 members who have a right to express their vote under the democratic process," Senator Carroll declared. And Morse said of the monitors' supervision: "They have already done it for two years. I think on the basis of what we know about the case so far, that is too long."

In the House of Representatives some Members were downright unkind in their candid illusions to the financial aspects of the monitorship. Congressman Abraham Multer of New York said: "It seems to me that the only reason that the court could have approved that kind of an arrangement is because there was some awfully nice patronage involved to the extent of $700,000 a year. The money comes from the union funds." Representative James Roosevelt mentioned impeachment in the same sentence with a reference to the Federal Judge in charge.

Congressman Frank Osmers of New Jersey said the interplay between Judge Letts, the monitors and the union was ". . . reaching comic opera proportions." Congressman John Shelley of California, a Teamster himself who had opposed Hoffa's elevation to the presidency, said there was no longer any necessity for the monitors. Congressman Elmer Holland of Pennsylvania charged the monitors were milking $2500 per day from the Teamsters treasury. Other Members joined in and had a field day at the expense of the good Judge and the Board of Monitors. The substance of their many thousands of words was, put an end to the Board of Monitors and call a convention.

Sidney Zagri, his great frame squeezed into one of the narrow seats in the Visitor's Gallery, looked pleased. He was witnessing the coup de grace of the monitors three and he knew it. He could practically see the mighty influence of fifteen Representatives and Senators oozing up the hallways, through the doors, down the Capitol

133

steps, across the Mall and up the court house steps on Third Street. It was only a matter of time, July 3, to be exact, for that was the date set for the convention following Judge Letts' order dissolving the Board of Monitors.

Jimmy Hoffa said recently of Sidney Zagri, "He's a hard worker and he's sincere," which is about as far as he has been known to go in praising anybody. But it would be difficult to believe that he does not have great faith in his Legislative Counsel. Zagri, in turn, admires and trusts Hoffa. When he first went to Washington from St. Louis several years ago he assured his teen-aged daughters that if he found Mr. Hoffa to be anything like he was pictured by Bobby Kennedy, the McClellan Committee and the press, he would resign immediately. His girls reminded him of his pledge every now and then when the committee hearings were running wild. "I think it would be easier to perjure yourself in front of a judge and jury than to lie into the clear eyes of a young girl," Sid Zagri has said.

Jimmy's relationship with some other staff members has become strained in recent years. This is expressed notably in the case of his former closest aides, Harold Gibbons and Lawrence Steinberg. Gibbons went to Washington after a successful job of building and running an important Local in St. Louis to serve as Hoffa's Executive Assistant. Larry Steinberg, once very friendly, was Hoffa's "personal representative," in fact, Jimmy's number one trouble-shooter. Both are intelligent, clean-cut, and came through the McClellan Committee ordeal with hardly a blemish.

Apparently the discontent had been smouldering for a long time before it broke into the open shortly after the tragedy of President Kennedy's assassination. A news story in the ultra-reliable *Wall Street Journal* sent a ripple through labor, management and political circles when it reported that Gibbons and Steinberg had resigned following a stormy session with Hoffa. Mentioning, anonymously, the ever-present rumors that Jimmy might be sacked by his Executive Board because of his personal troubles, the newspaper account said the straw that broke the camel's back was a petty argument over whether or not to close down the Teamster headquarters for a day of mourning the late President. Gibbons and Steinberg wanted to do so but Jimmy refused, the story said.

The report was correct in its visible aspects. The Teamsters building did not shut down for a day of mourning. Gibbons and Steinberg did resign their posts with the International, although both were to return from time to time for short stays to lend a hand during Jimmy's time-consuming trials in Chattanooga and Chicago.

Perhaps the most devastating thing about the entire affair from Jimmy's point of view, which is not to say he was in the least crushed, was that it had to have been "leaked" on purpose by someone very much inside the Teamster family. And not many knew the details, in fact, he could count them on the fingers of one hand and then eliminate one or two. But he didn't talk about it very much. "They sent up a trial balloon," he said easily, "but it fell like a rock." His hidden intimation, which may or may not have been intentional, could be interpreted as an acknowledgement of a move within the Executive Board to dump him.

Gibbons had long suffered under the quick tongue and overpowering personality of his boss. Once he was reported to have grieved, "I am the highest paid office boy in the country." If the latter part of his statement was true the former most certainly was for he was earning $30,000 per year frosted by a wide-open expense account. A man has to feel pretty strongly to quit a job like that, and Gibbons did. He yearned for more responsibility in the vital area of union-employer relations, particularly in contract negotiations which involved broad economic

135

problems, thousands of men and women, and millions of dollars. Unfortunately for his ambitions this was Jimmy's private preserve.

In Steinberg he found a kindred spirit and no doubt the two thought and talked long and hard before bucking Jimmy. Surely they knew that with Hoffa there was not and never could be room enough for anybody else at the top. Under present circumstances one can only surmise that both men have very "iffy" futures in the higher echelons of the Teamsters' Union. If Jimmy successfully appeals the convictions now clouding his own future, and if he is re-elected General President at the next convention, it would seem to be in the natural order of things for him to reappraise his lower level leadership, which is a nice way of saying—heads will roll.

In another, well-publicized incident in the internal affairs of the International, Sam Baron, a fourth-level official, walked into the court house one day sporting a black eye and a few cuts and bruises and swore out a warrant charging Jimmy with assault. He said he had borne the brunt of a temper tantrum by the barrel-chested Teamster boss. According to Jimmy this is what really happened:

"Sam came into my office under the influence. I said, 'Sam, if you get drunk anymore around here, you're fired.' He left my office mumbling something I couldn't understand. A few minutes later I walked into the conference room and he came at me from behind the door, made some remarks, and took a punch at me. Now I know Baron is an old man, fifty-nine, I believe, I simply pushed him away and he stumbled over a chair and went down. He got up and took another poke at me. I couldn't help admiring his spunk. I pushed him down without hitting him. Some of the other fellows came in and grabbed him and shoved him out into the hall. That's the last I saw of him."

The Government couldn't find any witnesses to back up Baron's assault story and the case was dropped—for the time being. Sid Zagri brought it up again in 1964 at the Democratic and Republican political conventions.

Zagri went to the Platform Committees of both parties to urge laws to prevent the Attorney General from employing *agent provocateurs* to try to trap labor leaders, specifically, Jimmy Hoffa. He produced a letter and inter-office memorandum on *Life* magazine letterheads proving that the Sam Baron case had been a put-up job. But neither party was interested. There were no votes to be had by defending Jimmy Hoffa.

There are two keys to Jimmy Hoffa's unshakable popularity among rank and file (what a worn-out term!) Teamsters. First is his single-minded attention to wages, hours, and working conditions in contrast to other well-known union leaders who like to talk about great national and international problems. Secondly, he has been made a martyr by the nation's press which, responding to the Kennedy's strategy, made him the number one bad boy of labor despite the strong likelihood that he is no better nor worse than the rest of them. People who work with their hands and backs aren't especially receptive to the high-sounding, self-righteous intonements of editorial pages geared to another world, and they are likely to take an opposite view.

"I am a member of Local 592, Truck Drivers and Helpers Union, which is part of the Teamsters' International Union. I am very proud to be a member of this labor movement," wrote Guy Kidd to the editor of the Richmond *Times-Dispatch,* January 11, 1963.

Guy Kidd could win first prize in a "Mr. Teamster" contest. He is a big six-footer with sandy, graying, receding hair. He has a heavy trunk, thick arms and hard hands. When he works he sweats. He is friendly and talkative and his phrases are laced with the idiom of the Appalachian Mountains from whence he came.

Guy Kidd's life in Virginia, a state which operates regally with fond memories of the old Confederacy in the east and less fondness for Federal revenue agents in the west where moonshining remains an important mainstay of the economy while coal mining and agriculture have declined. Guy came from the west. As a boy there he had worked on the farm; hard, honest, unproductive labor. As a young man he found employment in a hosiery mill and became an expert knitter; not with two needles, but with a great machine that turned out dozens of ladies' stockings at a "run."

He learned about labor unions in the army where he was a combat engineer, serving in both Germany and the Philippines during the fierce fighting of World War II. There was no union of soldiers, but he had a buddy, a Pennsylvanian, who had worked in a hosiery mill, too, and their jobs had been identical. But his buddy had earned a dollar an hour while he had earned only sixty cents. This came as a big surprise to Guy and he pondered it on many dark and lonely nights as he lay in the rain soaked jungle, eyes and ears alert to the dark perimeter of his company area, but with his mind dancing in the hills of Virginia. The only difference he could find between his and his buddies jobs was that his buddy belonged to a union. This was something to think about.

When he got back to the mountains, a "ruptured duck" discharge emblem in the lapel of his khaki uniform and that precious honorable discharge in his pocket, he returned to his old job in the hosiery mill. It still wasn't organized and although he thought about it often, he was not an impulsive man, and the boss had let it be known that he would shut down before he'd operate with a union in the mill.

Guy Kidd eventually quit his job at the mill. It didn't pay enough to let him support his family and he thought he could do better some place else. For a while he worked as a plumber, then as an electrician's helper and then as a dairy farm hand. He turned to mining for a while, joined the United Mine Workers' Local 132 and soon was elected its president, a position of small honor and no renumeration. The mine shut down, the Local was dissolved, and Guy returned to day labor.

In the mountain and farm areas of western and southside Virginia they have a saying about education: "Learn reading, 'riting, and the road to Richmond—that's the three R's," they laconically advise the young folks. Maybe Guy Kidd's early education came back to him for he set out for the big city.

A few weeks later he landed a job as a part-time checker in the Richmond terminal of the Mason-Dixon Lines, an east coast trucker. A few weeks more and he was a permanent, full-time employee and a member of Teamsters Local 592.

Guy went to work at one o'clock in the afternoon and got off at nine-thirty in the evening, five days a week. If he worked overtime he was paid "time and a half." He was guaranteed hospitalization insurance, life insurance, a pension plan and a paid vacation. Altogether the "fringe benefits" came to about fifty-seven cents an hour. His annual pay was more than $6300.00. Guy sent for his wife and children and they settled down into a quiet community in Richmond. This was home.

Perhaps Guy Kidd is more introspective than the average laboring man. In any event, he was acutely aware that now for the first time in twenty-five years he had a good job and security, and he attributed these improved circumstances to the Teamster-negotiated contract with his employers.

139

Guy Kidd was not disinterested in the world around him. He made a point of keeping up with community and national news and to that end read the daily newspaper carefully over a last pipe before going to work every day.

On January 8, 1963, he read an editorial in the *Times-Dispatch* that struck him as being all wrong. In fact, it made his blood boil. Entitled "The Power to Paralyze" the editorial asked the question: "How much longer will Congress tolerate the uncurbed power of unions to cripple the nation's industries, transportation, and communications?" Guy Kidd, who had never participated in a strike nor even witnessed one, read on. About mid-way down the column "Hoffa's Teamsters" were cited and indicted, not for what they had done, but for what they might do. And the editorial ended with instructions to Congress to outlaw "crippling strikes of regional or national scope."

Guy Kidd sat down to write a letter to the editor. This is what he wrote:

Dear Editor:

I am a member of Local 592, Truck Drivers and Helpers Union, which is a part of the Teamsters' International Union. I am proud to be a member of this labor movement. There is scarcely a day that passes but what I see an attack on Jimmy Hoffa, or some of the other members of the union family, in the newspapers or other means of news communications.

I will make no attempt to defend Mr. Hoffa on legal issues as he seems quite able to do this on his own. It is only natural in his fight for the Teamsters that he has made many enemies in high places. When some of these mighty people raise their voices they are heard the nation over and public opinion falls right behind the mighty.

In contrast, let some worker raise his voice in a complaint in a small terminal and see how little attention this gets in the nation's press. We here in this city have seen cases where the workers have agreed in National Labor Relations Board elections to join the Teamsters but the companies have refused to allow them to do so. They have forced men out on picket lines, trying to get the union of their choice to represent them.

The companies, firm believers in freedom of choice that they are, would be only too glad to allow the men to join a union if it would be the union that the company approves. In many cases they win by keeping men off jobs until some of the work crew returns, and then, with the help of our infamous "right-to-work" law, they hire a bunch of scabs to replace the workers who were the firm believers in a freedom-of-choice selection.

These workers are only asking for the same rights that I have, along with the majority of the workers in the interstate trucking industry. I get a proud check each week. I work hard to get this check. I am proud to go to any store in town and pay for my purchase with it. The businessman is proud to get it, for today I am able to say, "Make that portion of beef a little larger," or, "Get a better grade of clothing, we can afford it."

The real estate man is proud of our checks, for with them we are buying nice property, building nice homes, having enough leisure time to putter around the house and keep them looking good while paying taxes and helping to make our neighborhood a better place to live.

I am also proud to be working for a company that is fair in its dealings with us. I am indeed proud to cash the check that has imprinted on it "This is motor truck money," for it shows that a union and a company can get along and both of them help their communities by fulfilling their duties to each other.

Then Guy Kidd signed his name. On the way to work he mailed the letter.

If the editors and the Congressmen and Bobby Kennedy looking down from their ivory towers would take the time to read Guy Kidd's letter, and if they could understand it which is not at all certain, they might gain some insight into the strength of the labor union movement as well as Jimmy Hoffa's personal popularity among his union constituents.

Jimmy Hoffa is a Teamster to the very marrow in his bones and the members can feel it in theirs. He identifies with them and he socializes with them. "I get a lot of invitations from employers, go here, go there. I don't go. If I want to go duck hunting I go with my stewards, my business agents. In Florida there's always ten, fifteen employers want me to use their boats. I don't need 'em. We got our own boat. I go with my own people, where I belong."

To Jimmy the Union is combined life and love: "I average from twelve to fifteen hours a day, six or seven days a week. I like this job. I like to represent the individuals I represent. Every hour I work is an hour of pleasure, and the hours disappear like magic.

"I have had experience with General Presidents who have lost touch with the members and I am a firm believer that being in a building like this—six and a half million dollars and the luxurious surroundings—meeting with the important people who come in and out of this building— very conceivably you can forget where you came from."

"I have no desire to forget where I came from. I am not ashamed of my background. I am proud of it."

CHAPTER 12

Bobby Gets His Man (Maybe)

The Federal Government has made six major efforts to put Jimmy behind bars. The first three were clear-cut victories for Jimmy and humiliating, personal defeats for Bobby Kennedy because he chose to make the contests personal. (He said he'd jump off the Capitol dome if he didn't get a conviction.) These were the bribery case which ended in an acquittal, a wiretapping case tried twice, once to a hung jury and the second time an acquittal.

In May, 1962 Jimmy was indicted in Nashville, Tennessee on charges of accepting payments from an employer in violation of the Taft-Hartley Act. Specifically, Jimmy and his friend and fellow Teamster Owen Bert Brennan had set up a truck leasing firm which had supplied equipment to Commercial Carriers, Incorporated, a Detroit company specializing in hauling new cars from factory to dealers. The leasing firm, called Test Fleet, Incorporated, was owned by the wives of the two labor leaders in their maiden names, Josephine Poszywak and Alice Johnson.

Jimmy insisted there was nothing wrong in owning a trucking company and admitted being interested in a number of trucking and related enterprises. "I once heard of a doctor that had a piece of an undertaking firm," he said wryly. "Some of his professional patients later became his business patrons, but nobody accused him of anything wrong." And he brushed off the fact that his share was in his wife's name, although the Government made much of it. "I know a lot of guys put property in their wives' names. I hear women own most of the wealth in this country. I happen to be the husband of Mrs. Hoffa."

But the Government was not to be thrown off the track by such simple, one-sided logic. They found witnesses who said Commercial Carriers had to do business with Test Fleet in order to prevent labor disputes. Bobby Kennedy, now the Attorney General of the United States, set a whole battery of Justice Department lawyers and staff to work on the case. Their preparation was meticulous. The trial lasted two months and ended in a mistrial due to a hung jury. Most of the jurors, it later developed, had been for acquittal. The vote had been seven to five when they gave up. But that wasn't the end of the Test Fleet case by a long shot. On May 9, 1963 Jimmy and six others were indicted on charges of jury tampering in connection with it.

(Jimmy's personal courage was put to test during the Test Fleet trial when an unemployed dishwasher stalked into the Nashville court room, past a dozen or so U. S. Marshals and FBI men, and, drawing an air-powered pellet gun from his clothing quickly pumped three shots into Jimmy at point-blank range. The marshals, witnesses and attorneys on both sides hit the floor. Jimmy went for his assailant, catching him on the jaw with a straight, hard right knocking him to the floor. The would-be assassin said he intended to kill Jimmy in answer to "a message from a higher power." "I know it sounds crazy," he added.)

The jury tampering trial began in January, 1964, in the ornate third floor court room of the Federal Building in Chattanooga, Judge Frank W. Wilson, presiding. Judge Wilson looked boyishly young at forty-seven. His dark, wavy hair combed back from his high forehead lent to a striking Barrymoresque profile. He had been appointed to the bench by President John F. Kennedy after a successful career practicing law during which he also practiced local, Democratic politics. The proceedings were routine and rather boring until February 4, when the Government trotted in its hitherto secret, star witness. This witness, one Edward Grady Partin, *was* the trial.

There are two Edward Partins. One is the man the jury saw and heard. So far as they knew in the course of the trial he was a Teamster Union official, president of a Baton Rouge, Louisiana Local, a former intimate of Jimmy and other high ranking Teamster leaders who sickened and finally turned informer to ease his conscience and to aid his Government in the cause of justice.

The other Edward Partin, so carefully hidden from the jury, is recorded for posterity in criminal records from coast to coast from 1943 when he was convicted on a breaking and entering charge until late 1962 when he was indicted for first-degree manslaughter. In between his record shows:

A bad conduct discharge from the Marine Corps;

Indictment for kidnapping;

A charge of raping a young Negro girl;

Indictment on embezzlement and falsifying records charges;

Indictment for forgery;

A charge of conspiring with one of Castro's generals to smuggle arms into Cuba, all of which was discussed during the trial but never in the presence of the jury. Judge Wilson ruled dozens of times that Partin's character had no bearing in the evaluation of his word against that of the defendants.

Partin's conflicts with law and order rendered him very newsworthy in his native State and consequently his more recent escapades are easily traced through news accounts. In November, 1961 he was involved in a mysterious shooting incident which left him with a .38 caliber slug in the abdomen. He assured police the gun went off accidentally while he was fooling around with it. They had a notion it might have something to do with his continuing, sometimes bloody, fight with members of the Teamsters Local where several had accused him of embezzling union funds and conspiring to aid Castro.

Partin's principal accusers, J. D. Albin and A. G. Klein, Jr., were badly beaten by six of his friends. Soon after, a truck load of sand defied the laws of physics to fall upon Klein, killing him instantly.

This series of unhappy events came to the attention of the Justice Department resulting in a thorough investigation and Partin's indictment on twenty-six counts. He went free on $50,000 bail. The potential consequences of the multiple indictment could amount to fines of $260,-000 and seventy-eight years in a Federal prison. But this was only the beginning.

Six months earlier, on Christmas Day, 1961, somebody ran down a young soldier's car, killing one and seriously injuring two others, and then took off down the highway at a high rate of speed. A painstaking investigation led to Partin's indictment on charges of first-degree manslaughter and leaving the scene of an accident.

The day before the above cited indictment Partin walked into the court house under his own power and gave himself up on yet another serious charge; kidnapping. This involved a little favor he'd done for a friend who was separated from his wife who had legal custody of their two children. Both Partin and his friend were booked for kidnapping and the children were still missing. Two weeks after his surrender the children appeared and Partin became eligible for bail on the manslaughter charge.

This exhausting recitation of events, seemingly unrelated to Jimmy Hoffa, is in fact very much related. Partin's original $50,000 bond had been revoked when his other problems came to the attention of the bonding company but now, like magic, it was renewed with some to spare to cover all indictments. Partin walked out of jail and straight into a telephóne booth to call his boss in the Teamsters' Union, Jimmy Hoffa. Known to him but unknown to Jimmy, his new found friends of the Justice Department were on hand with their wiretapping devices to take down on tape every word that was spoken. Partin told Jimmy in this and a later call, also recorded, that he wanted to talk to him about his problems. He said the Justice Department was persecuting him; an approach guaranteed to strike a sympathetic chord in Jimmy; while they were sitting beside him listening in. Jimmy said he was going to be tied up in Nashville for a few days. Partin claimed he was invited to Nashville. Jimmy insisted he invited himself. In any event, he went.

Why would Jimmy have anything to do with the likes of Edward Partin? Was it because they were fellow crooks? Not at all, Jimmy asserts: "We've got over 900 Locals and at least three times that many local officers, all elected by local members. I have to deal with the duly elected officers whether I like them or don't like them. If the Landrum-Griffin law don't bar a man from holding office, I can't bar him. Partin said he wanted to talk to me about problems concerning the Local. I'm always available for that. That's my job."

Before departing for Nashville Partin had conversations with Justice Department agents. These were Baton Rouge District Attorney Sargent Pitcher and his gum-shoe, William (the Hawk) Daniels, Frank Grimsley and Walter Sheridan, Bobby's man on the spot. Sheridan had been an investigator for the old McClellan Committee and had gone with Bobby to the Justice Department when he became his brother's Attorney General. There he was put in charge of the special unit known as the Hoffa Brigade. Briefed by these experts Partin was to go to Nashville and "if I saw evidence of jury tampering or other illegal activities" to report to Sheridan.

Proceeding according to plan he arrived in Nashville just in the nick of time to receive some hot jury tampering information from a gentleman he met for the first time in the lobby of the Andrew Jackson Hotel where Jimmy and his entourage were staying. This man, who turned out to be Nicholas J. Tweel, a friend of a friend of Jimmy, told Partin he had come to town to help set up a method to get to the jury. This information was promptly passed on to Sheridan and later related in court.

Partin stayed in Nashville throughout the Test Fleet case, remaining in close touch with Walter Sheridan and passing on information which was to be the foundation of the Government's charges of jury tampering against Jimmy and five others. This is the trial that began in Chattanooga on January 20, 1964, in Judge Wilson's court. The defendants, besides Hoffa, were: Ewing King, former president of Teamsters' Local 327 in Nashville; Nicholas J. Tweel, a West Virginia busnessman; Allen Dorfman, a Chicago insurance broker and close business friend of Jimmy; Thomas E. Parks, a Nashville funeral home employee; and, Larry Campbell, a business agent of Local 299 in Detroit. Each defendant had his own attorney.

Judge Wilson and the defense attorneys had a mild skirmish on the very first day when Campbell's lawyer, Cecil Branstetter, objected to the composition of the list of prospective jurors which he found top-heavy with classes of people he felt might be unfavorably disposed toward his client. He said the list contained too few blue-collar, working class people and too many white collar, semi professional, Civil Service, and others who might likely look down their noses at common, laboring, union people. Jacques Schiffer, representing Parks, said he had tried to get the list of veniremen far enough in advance to study it but had received it only the day before. However, after considerable debate Judge Wilson, in his patient, preoccupied manner, overruled the protests. The jury was selected and the trial proceeded.

The prosecution, not unethically, sought to depict the defendants as arrogant, ruthless, fast operators, who lived on the outer fringes of the law, contemptuous of the American jury system. A series of witnesses told, under careful examination by Government attorneys, of startling and bizarre efforts to influence the Nashville jury. They mentioned large dollar figures, job promotions, and political influence. They spoke of shadowy approaches usually late at night on dark, lonely roads, often in the rain.

Upon cross-examination by defense counsel these wild and complicated tales more or less fell apart and observers agreed that Hoffa was a lead pipe cinch to get out of this one, too. Jimmy was confident. On February 3 he assured a friend he would meet him in Florida two weeks hence for some fishing and a few days of rest and relaxation.

In retrospect it seems apparent that the early days of the trial were just so much window-dressing designed to create an atmosphere of intrigue and confusion before the appearance of the main witness, Edward Grady Partin. When he walked into the courtroom the defense was completely surprised, even stunned, while the prosecution was suddenly smilingly eager and confident.

Partin's testimony was barely underway—he had just had time to tell about his initial meeting with Tweel when the latter, who, ironically and contradictorily, was one of only two of the six defendants to be acquitted, confided plans to fix the jury—when defense cousel moved to supress his entire testimony.

149

James E. Haggerty, former president of the Michigan Bar Association and attorney for defendant Hoffa, argued that Partin had been planted as an undercover agent to spy on the defense at Nashville in an "improper intrusion on the defendant's right." Soft spoken, grandfatherly, owlish-eyed Haggerty had a tone of hurt and sorrow as he told Judge Wilson: "He (Partin) was in discussion, I might tell you, with lawyers. He had had discussions with me during the trial of the case and to my knowledge discussions with others. He was constantly hanging around. I never knew for what reason. He was in court . . . he was at the hotel and Mr. Hoffa's suite where the lawyers conferred at night."

Slim, ascetic Harvey M. Silets, attorney of Allen Dorfman, claimed such spying on the defense was illegal. It was, he declared, "As if Your Honor's law clerk should all of a sudden turn out to be an informer and a spy for the defense." Silets recalled that during the Nashville trial the prosecutor, James Neal, had assured the judge there was no eavesdropping, no wire tap, no evidence illegally obtained, obviously knowing all the time of Partin's two-faced role.

Upon cross-examination Partin could not remember hearing anything about the trial while he was hanging around the hotel suite crowded with the defendants and their attorneys although he recalled in minutest detail conversations with defendants and others regarding alleged jury tampering. In one reply he said with a straight face that he "wasn't interested in the case."

William Bufalino, a Detroit lawyer and Teamster and an old associate of Jimmy, took the stand. He had been present throughout the Nashville trial. "I was in the process of preparing, interviewing several witnesses, truck drivers . . . I asked questions and I made notes. These notes were typed in question and answer form. . . . They were typed and Ed Partin helped me staple them. He was carrying copies back and forth from one place to another." Also, Partin had been present during an evening strategy session when an outline of the following day's tactics was formulated:

"The next day when I got on this particular area I started, now, and this is the language, 'Now, witness, I bring you back to 1953,' and that is all I had to say and Mr. Neal jumped to his feet and said, 'I object, Your Honor, they are getting into a different area.'

"I said, 'How do you know where I am going, what I am going to ask?' He answered, and he said, 'Your Honor, I suggest, may I request, that the jury leave this room and I want to argue this particular case in the absence of the jury.' The jury left, left the court room.

"I said to Mr. Neal, 'How do you know what I am going to ask, all I said was 1953?'

"He said, 'I am psychic.'

"That is in the record."

James Neal did not bother to rebut Bufalino's testimony but Walter Sheridan testified that Partin did in fact pass on information pertaining to the trial. Defense tried to prove that Partin was not just another Teamster hanging around to do business with Hoffa, nor a friend invited to visit, but rather, was a paid spy; an *agent provocateur*. Bufalino testified to an incident of "baiting" by Partin:

"I have some recollection that Partin said something about a particular juror, I don't know which one, that he was in the army with one and he was starting to suggest that maybe he should get in touch with that fellow. . . .

"I said, 'Look, I want to have absolutely nothing to do at all with any such discussion. Lay off that. We have a cinch case. This case is absolutely nothing. And then, so far as I'm concerned, I suggest you just forget about anything like that.'"

Silets questioned Partin regarding the instructions he received from "The Hawk" Daniels and Frank Grimsley, seeking to establish that he had been *sent* to Nashville for the sole and specific purpose of trapping Jimmy. Judge Wilson sustained Neal's objections to this line of questioning. "I have difficulty in seeing how it is material to the issue that is now before the court," he said in a detached way, without looking up from his note-taking.

Partin doggedly denied that he had been paid anything by the Government and was backed up by prosecution witnesses. (This was categorically refuted, but later in the trial, when defense proved beyond question that the Justice Department, through a circuitous route, funneled at least one thousand, five hundred dollars to Mrs. Partin.)

But the Judge found in favor of the prosecution. Defenses's motion to supress Partin's testimony was denied. ". . . I cannot understand, frankly speaking, with all due respect, that Your Honor has reached his conclusion," Mr. Haggerty quietly remarked, quietly laying groundwork for appeal.

Back on the stand, this time with the jury in the box, Partin was put through his paces by Government lawyers. He said he heard Hoffa remark after some damaging testimony, "I would pay $15,000 or $20,000, whatever it costs, to get to the jury." In reference to an attempt to bribe that failed, Jimmy supposedly said: "The dirty bastard went in told the Judge. . . . We are going to have to lay low a few days."

Partin said he ran into King and Hoffa one day in the hallway and stood by while they talked. Jimmy was "raising cain" he said, and quoted him as saying, "he keeps telling me he can get the patrolman, but he don't get him."

Once he commented to Jimmy that the trial didn't seem to be going so well, and Jimmy replied, he said: "Don't worry about it too much because I have got the colored juror in my hip pocket. One of my business agents, Campbell, came into Nashville prior to the trial and took care of it."

On cross examination, Hoffa's Chattanooga counsel, Harry Berke, was quick to leap onto the most obvious error in Partin's testimony:

Q. Didn't you say this, Mr. Partin, speaking about Mr. Hoffa, he said, "One of my business agents, Campbell, came to Nashville prior to the trial and took care of it?"

A. That's correct. That is exactly what I said. You are right.

Q. How could he fix the jury prior to the time when he didn't know who was going to be on it?

Partin looked toward the prosecution's table where James Neal was on his feet shouting an objection. Court room spectators were dumbfounded when Judge Wilson sustained it.

The defense tried to bring out testimony relating to Partin's character claiming it a vital factor since it was one man's word against another's. In addition to his criminal record, there was a letter from a Cuban general thanking the ex-Marine for his help in training Castro's militia. And there was the matter of plotting to run arms and ammunition to the blockaded Communist stronghold. This entire line of inquiry was blocked by Neal's objections sustained by Judge Wilson's rulings. The Judge and the prosecutor had an incredible rapport. At least once an objection was sustained before it was made.

Silets was questioning Partin. The colloquy went like this:

Q. You have pleaded guilty to other offenses, haven't you?

A. Minor fighting or something.

Q. And one of those was assaulting a Mr. Colotto which you plead guilty to on December 5, 1955?

Judge Wilson: "Sustain the objection."

Mr. Silets: "I didn't hear one, Your Honor."

Judge Wilson: "Well, counsel stood up."

James Haggerty was incredulous. "In my forty-one years of experience, mostly in Federal courts, I have witnessed an exhibition this morning . . . that leave me clearly puzzled and somewhat disgusted." He did not say this privately to a colleague, but publicly, in a court room, to Judge Frank W. Wilson.

The trial took a turn toward the bizarre with the appearance of Frederick Michael Shobe for the defense. Shobe had served a prison term for armed robbery, burglary and forgery. Out on parole he was picked up for associating with some bad characters, but, instead of being returned to jail he made a deal with the Justice Department to work for Walter Sheridan as an undercover agent in the "Hoffa Brigade." (Although this writer was shocked to learn of such arrangement, apparently it goes on all the time.) After two years, and in keeping with the promise of eventually having the opportunity to pick up a normal life, he was offered a job in Japan. Resenting what he interpreted as an attempt to hustle him out of the country, he told all to William Bufalino. Why Bufalino, a Teamster official? Because for the two years of his employment by the Justice Department he had been acting the role of *agent provocateur,* stirring up trouble in Teamster units all over the country.

On the witness stand Shobe testified to his long and close association with Sheridan. He told of being sent to Detroit with instructions to find "someone who would state that Larry Campbell and Charles O'Brien had made incriminating statements about their interest in the Hoffa trial." In spite of rapid-fire objections by the prosecution

154

which were invariably upheld by the Judge, Shobe unfolded an incredible tale. However, the Judge dismissed the jury and this evidence went unheard except by courtroom personnel and a handful of spectators.

Shobe told of discussing defendant Thomas Parks with Sheridan. Since Parks earned only about $1500 per year they realized they might have a problem figuring out where he got money to offer anybody as a bribe. Somehow, some cash would have to be traced from Jimmy to him. It was Shobe's job to dig up the evidence. He systematically ran down a list of Parks' friends and associates supplied by Sheridan looking for a lead. At last he came upon one Bishop St. Psalm, a Nashville voodoo merchant and practitioner, who indicated he might cooperate to the extent of casting a spell on Parks if somebody would oblige by buying advertising in a little magazine he published. Shobe didn't have much confidence in voodoo but Sheridan said they might as well try it, Nashville being a city of many superstitious people. Assured of the advertising the Bishop went to work. He visited the little shack where Tom Parks was trying to get established in a cleaning and pressing business and picked up a few of his personal possessions which he proceeded to "curse" with mystical incantations in the presence of black, burning candles, which was supposed to put a hex on Parks making him amenable to Government agents.

Jacques Schiffer questioned Shobe:

Q. Let me ask you this now: As you sit here now can you tell us whether you had discussed with Walter Sheridan a plan to frame Mr. Hoffa?

A. We had discussed Mr. Hoffa, Mr. Bufalino and Mr. Fitzsimmons and various Teamster officials . . . as a matter of fact, this was a constant topic, it was my understanding that the only reason for the existence of the particular department that Walter headed was to get Mr. Hoffa.

Q. I see. Was that made plain to you by Walter Sheridan that the purpose was to get Hoffa?

A. That is correct.

Q. And was it indicated to you that it made no difference whether he was— — —, they used legal or illegal means?

A. Well, preferably if there was something found that incriminated Mr. Hoffa, well and good; however, if there wasn't, the feeling in the department was that Mr. Hoffa should be in jail anyway and that we — —, if we had to resort to unfair tactics, well, that's where a person like myself came in.

Q. I see. And that is why they called you into service because they wanted you, like you described, "that's why they wanted me in the service, to frame Hoffa," is that correct?

A. Well, to get him by any means, fair or foul, that was my understanding of the matter.

Q. And you were directly told that by Walter Sheridan?

A. That is correct.

Shobe told of plans to kidnap and scare Tom Parks. They talked of picking him up in a phony arrest, handcuffing, gaging and blindfolding him and taking him to a lonely spot in the woods far out of the city. They would have a couple of spades and would start digging a hole . . . "I imagine he would get the message." They went so far with this melodramatic plot as to figure out how to have men rush onto the scene, just in the nick of time, to save Parks after he was sufficiently frightened to want to cooperate with Hoffa's enemies.

But the jury heard none of this testimony. With his damaging testimony blocked out by the prosecution's objections and the Judge's upholding decisions, Shobe's testimony that finally reached the jury was of so little consequence that the Government neither challenged nor rebutted it.

There remained one final explosion to mushroom above the bar of justice in Chattanooga. This was triggered by James Haggerty, whose urgent, outraged tones seemed out of character in contrast with his normal quietness, when he reported to the Judge (perhaps accused him) that the defense had proof of constant surveillance by Government agents. He submitted as evidence a photograph "taken last night" of an FBI agent spying on the defense. Such surveillance, Haggerty said, was not casual, but active, and it "hamstrings the defendants and the defendants' counsel."

Schiffer lit into the prosecution. His debate with Neal degenerated into a bitter, personal argument. Claiming his telephone was tapped he asked Judge Wilson to put Neal on the stand and "let him say under oath that there has been no surveillance in this case, not anything to the effect, "I know of none." Neal said he would gladly testify that "to the best of my knowledge and belief" but that wasn't good enough for the fiery attorney. But nothing, of course, came of this heated discussion.

On the afternoon of the same day Schiffer returned to the courtroom after the luncheon recess to report that his files had been looted. Haggerty said he had seen the files and could vouchsafe some of the important trial documents were missing. Also, Haggerty said, his law clerk had been shadowed while on an errand bearing on the trial and a door in the suite occupied by the Hoffa party had been jimmied. "Now, how can we try a case under these Gestapo tactics?" he asked the Judge, who went on making notes on his yellow, lined legal pad. He would not, he reiterated, take up the matter of surveillance until later.

When Jimmy Hoffa took the stand in his own defense he was fighting one man—Edward Partin. Nobody else had come close to linking him with jury tampering attempts and it was one man's word against another's. Unfortunately Partin's character as reflected by his active career in crime had no bearing on the jury simply because they didn't know of it. Jimmy's character, as reflected by the public image in turn reflecting McClellan Committee press releases and public statements by Bobby Kennedy and others, was well established with the general public, not excluding jurors no matter how non-biased they are supposed to be.

Jimmy testified that Partin's story was "an absolute lie," generally and specifically. Yes, he had been present at the Andrew Jackson Hotel during most of the trial. He had come there on his own initiative to discuss with the Teamsters' Union General President his problems as president of a Teamsters' Local Union. While in the vicinity of the Hoffa suite and elsewhere the defendants and their attorneys congregated he was bound to have overheard discussions regarding the jury—defendants and their lawyers just naturally talk about the jury and they speak in the idiom. Such talk might very well be misinterpreted by a layman.

Jimmy was pretty well occupied with his own affairs and with Teamster business more pressing than that of the Baton Rouge Local, but when, near the end of the trial, he and Bufalino found time to sit down with Partin they saw him "upset, nervous and almost incoherent." He was "very perturbed" about his opposition among the membership of his local and charges about his ties with Fidel Castro. Jimmy asked him point-blank to confirm or deny these charges. Partin, Jimmy testified under oath, "tried to explain it away . . . as though it was just nothing."

Jimmy found the finances of Partin's local to be in terrible disorder due to mismanagement and squandering. Finally he told Partin to get his house in order, clear up the charges against him, or the International would have to take over under the trusteeship provision of the Teamster constitution. "He stormed out of the room and that is the way we left it," Jimmy swore.

The case went to the jury and Judge Wilson began hearing the arguments on the surveillance issue.

While the FBI was taking seven hundred and twenty-three candid photographs of just about everybody who came and went during the trial (including, no doubt, the suspicious character now pounding this typewriter), bugging conversations, shadowing the defendants, their attorneys, and other suspects, Jimmy imported his own counterspy. This was Bernard Spindel, an electronics expert who finds employment in "our naked society"[1] as a private investigator, agent, or counter-agent. Jacques Schiffer presented to Judge Wilson a sealed envelope containing twenty-nine pages of transcriptions of Spindel's recordings of the FBI's recordings, taken on the scene, for while they were spying on Jimmy, Spindel was spying on them with a recording machine that could pick their conversations out of the air waves. The Judge received the envelope as though it were doused in radio-active fallout, commenting disdainfully and some thought painfully that he wasn't familiar "with the practice of a stranger to a lawsuit filing a sealed document. . . ."

This really rankled the defense lawyers for earlier in the trial, when a vital issue was whether Partin had gone to Nashville on his own initiative or been invited by Jimmy, the Judge had in his possession transcripts of tape recordings received from the prosecution attorneys, recordings of Partin's telephone conversations with Jimmy proving the former.

When this came out later in the trial, too late to be effective in proving the *agent provocateur* claim by defense,

---

[1] "The Naked Society" by Vance Packard, David McKay Company, Inc., N. Y.

Judge Wilson blandly said he didn't know that defense didn't know he had the taped Partin-Hoffa conversations. In other words, he had sat there on the bench with full knowledge of the vital evidence and listened to the defense lawyers make fools of themselves trying to prove something they knew but had no evidence of. The prosecution also remained silent while Jimmy squirmed in frustration. Both James Neal and Judge Frank Wilson knew very well Partin was lying when he claimed in front of the jury to have been invited to Nashville. The recorded transcripts read, in part:

Partin: "Ah, what I was thinking, Jimmy, after I get this thing straightened out . . . I would like to get with you and talk this thing out."

Hoffa: "Well, I'll be here all week."

Partin: "I hate to interrupt you, Jim, but I need to talk to you . . . when can I see you?—you'd say you'd be there on the 22nd in Nashville? . . . Will Sunday or Monday be all right?"

Hoffa: "Right."

Jacques Schiffer, not surprisingly, found a double standard in the Judge's attitudes toward sealed envelopes offered by the prosecution and those offered by the defense.

While the surveillance issue was being debated the jury brought in its verdict. Jimmy was convicted along with Ewing King, Thomas Parks and Larry Campbell. Tweel and Dorfman were acquitted. On March 12, 1964, Jimmy was sentenced to eight years and fined $10,000. King, Parks and Campbell each received three year sentences and $5,000 fines. Jacques Schiffer, Parks' attorney, was charged (by the Judge) with "willful and criminal contempt" and sentenced to sixty days in jail and fined $1,000. In passing sentence on Jimmy the Judge made a brief statement that seems strangely out of place in the voluminous transcript of the trial, laced, as it is, with fascinating, sometimes revolting stories, of spying, intimidation, and suppressed evidence on the part of the Government, along with the childish, idiotic stories of voodoo and fakery. Judge Wilson said:

"You stand here convicted of seeking to corrupt the administration of justice itself. You stand here convicted of having tampered, really, with the very soul of this nation. You stand here convicted of having struck at the very foundation upon which everything else in this nation depends, the basis of civilization itself, and that is the administration of justice, because without a fair, proper and lawful administration of justice, nothing else would be possible in this country, the administration of labor unions, the administration of business, the carrying on of occupations, the carrying on of recreation, the administration of health services, everything that we call civilization depends ultimately upon the proper administration of justice itself."

Nothing came of the surveillance hearing in Judge Wilson's court but much was made of it in the appeals filed by Hoffa's attorneys on all counts.

* * * * *

In another trial, later in 1964, the Government once again tied Jimmy into a package with several co-defendants and lowered the boom. The way the Government saw it the eight defendants put together a sweet racket. The Central States Teamster Pension Fund is administered by eight employer and eight Teamster trustees including Jimmy. But, according to the Government, the eight employer representatives and seven other union men were just so many pawns in Jimmy's powerful hands and his word alone was sufficient to approve or disapprove a loan application. He was charged with influencing the other fifteen trustees to approve loans after referring the borrowers to one of the group of defendants who then referred the loan application back to the Fund where it was approved and whereupon he collected a fat finders fee.

The eight defendants were charged with demanding and receiving fees, stock options and stock interests as their compensation in obtaining loans. The indictment cited fourteen loans obtained for the financing of hotels, shopping centers, hospitals and other projects in several states.

The Government claimed that one purpose of the involved scheme was to secure funds to bail out Jimmy from personal financial involvement in Sun Valley, Inc., a Florida retirement homes development. They said $100,000 was diverted for this purpose.

All eight of the defendants, who, besides Jimmy, were: S. George Burris, Herbert R. Burris, Samuel Hyman, Calvin Kovens, Benjamin Dranow, Abe Weinblatt and Zachary A. Starke, Jr., were charged with twenty counts of mail fraud, seven counts of wire fraud, and one count of conspiracy to defraud the Pension Fund and to obtain money from the Fund through "false and fraudulent pretenses."

The long and tedious trial took place at Chicago during the summer of 1964, which, for James Hoffa was a long and a hot one. It ended in another conviction—five years and $10,000 fine—and another appeal. Jimmy is confident the appeal will be successful due to the hitherto discussed methods of the prosecution and the decade-long vendetta conducted by Robert Kennedy, irregularities in the trial procedures, but mainly due to the fact that he is not guilty.

CHAPTER 13

The Hoffa Mind and Idiom

My daughter and my son finished college. It is the first generation for either a Hoffa or Poszywak, my wife's family, on her mother's, her father's, my mother's and my father's side to have had an opportunity to finish college. It is a great American institution that permits men like myself to come from a warehouse to here, my wife from a laundry to where she stands here today.

Personal contact is the key to service and giving the membership service is the only reason we are in business. That political and social stuff—it's not important. I don't think the drivers expect me to be holding social gatherings for them or to go on the air and tell what's wrong in Germany or Italy. Running a union is just like running a business. We're in the business of selling labor. We're going to get the best price we can.

I plan to work until I retire here at the Teamsters. I work hard because I like it. That's the only way. It is my pleasure to travel all around the United States, talking to our members, talking to the labor movement as a whole. In addition to that, I make it my business to at least once every ninety days conduct my own local union's membership meeting in Detroit. I make it my business to sit in on grievance meetings, negotiate contracts and generally administer the affairs of this International Union as I believe is for the best interests for all members.

There is ninety percent of this business you can't talk about. You have to have a lot of keys to operate a union like this. If you talk about it, it would hurt too many people.

You never look back on your life. You live every day today. I don't hold any grudge against John F. Kennedy. That was a propaganda stunt by some individuals trying to see how far they could push. When I didn't push they gave up. I am sorry he was assassinated. But the glorification that is taking place, taking place in the newspapers, taking place in television, history will put in its right place. He was a young man and he was learning. But the history books won't print what he might have done if he'd served out his term, maybe another term. It will print the facts that speak for themselves. He was a minority president, elected by less than fifty percent of the people that voted in that election. Right after he took his office was the Cuban invasion. He had to give the nod or it wouldn't have been done. He lost his nerve in the middle of the Bay of Pigs. That's not what Hoffa says, people don't like to think it, but that's what happened and that's what history will print. In Congress he didn't get anything on his legislative program. It took Johnson to get Congress to move and history will have to print it that way. The only thing going for him is getting Khruschev to pull missiles out of Cuba in 1962 and the whole story there is not yet known. What did he promise Khrushchev? It looks like he promised to let Castro alone. I don't know but history will find out and tell what nobody is telling now.

There are certain kinds of people in the labor movement who are bums. I think they are all interested in themselves politically, and for some reason I don't understand, they have a collective understanding not to make certain people look bad—certain people on Capitol Hill—

even though in the process they are destroying the effective power of organized labor. That's my belief. The AFL-CIO top leadership sold the labor movement down the river to save their own hides.

George Meany is the last person in the world who should be head of a union. He ought to get a great big mirror and stand in front of it and take a good look into it and see if he can stand the scrutiny that Hoffa has stood. But he answered better than anybody as to his own qualifications to be a leader. He proudly told the National Association of Manufacturers that he never negotiated an agreement, never organized a worker and never called a strike. Now if that's the qualifications for being a labor leader, then I don't qualify because I have negotiated contracts by the hundreds, I have signed up members by the thousands, and I've called strikes when I needed to.

When you're old and decrepit on top of being stupid, you're in trouble. Some day the man is going to come to the door and tell you you're out of business. But George Meany will never retire on his own decision as long as there's a breath of life in him. When he retires, it will be in a box. When that happens the one fellow who could take over the AFL-CIO would be Walter Reuther. I don't have to like a guy to say what's true. I recognize the fact that he runs a successful union. And he is currently up to date on the problems of this country and he is trying to do something about them, which is more than I can say for most people.

As this investigation started the Teamsters Union was picked because of their militant position, because of their participation in every strike in the country, because it is a strong union. Many of the employers that we deal with fought bitterly, stubbornly with every tool they could buy, whether it be a paid judge, a paid strikebreaker, or a controlled individual who governed trucks by administration. They fought and as they lost this battle they moved into the Congress. And when the McClellan Committee hearings started, many people spent hours of the night glued to the TV because it was a greater thriller than any one of the man-hunt programs on the air.

You had the great Senate of the United States with subpoena powers to reach out anywhere in the United States, pluck out an individual, insist that he grab an airplane, go to Washington and appear in front of this committee. He had to come without any knowledge of the questions he might be asked, without any right of having counsel cross-examine the witness against him, without any right of research to present a proper case, without any rules of law.

The only right was to appear there, sit there and be harassed, harangued and abused by individuals who professed to have labor at heart—men like McClellan, men like Mundt out of the Dakotas, men like Curtis out of Nebraska, individuals who never voted for a single thing that was decent for the working man.

They knew that an individual coming in there had violated no law, but this individual came there, and out of fear of being tricked by lawyers, out of fear of not being represented by counsel of his own choosing, he took the Fifth Amendment, which is a Constitutional right of Americans, he was again criticized and harangued and harassed by the chairman of the committee.[1]

Now for the first time in the United States there may go all the way to the Supreme Court of the United States a case very carefully prepared to determine whether any individual citizen of the United States has a right to a fair trial, has a right to investigate to learn the facts before the trial and whether he has a right to be represented by coun-

[1] Here Hoffa is referring to someone other than himself. He never took the Fifth Amendment.

sel with the courage to stand there and fight the Government.

Once and for all we will determine whether we are first, second or third class citizens. It is their desire to tear down individuals once they are indicted, to make them crawl and squirm, to make them live in fear prior to their trial. They want to crush us morally, mentally and financially.

I was brought up on the street and nobody is going to make me squirm, wiggle, twist or turn—to hell with them.

* * * *

I don't know what those new guys will do but that Khruschev was probably one of the smartest political leaders in the world and one of the trickiest. What he did was capitalize on sweet words, but their policy won't change and we will evenutally have trouble. They would be almost bankrupt but we have been fools and helped them out. This coexistence is like when you get a contract with an employer after a long, tough fight. He smiles at you across the table when he signs because you've whipped him and he can't do nothing else. But he stays in line just until he learns your tactics then he turns around and whips you. What he's done in the meantime is coexist. The only way you can avoid this is always be on the offensive. Don't let him get to know you, your tactics. Keep changing and keep pushing. That way he never gets to know you well enough to figure out how to beat you.

They are nuts if they think Russia and Red China won't get back together. We will lose all of Latin America. Why should any South American, Latin American country deal with us at arms length when we give them as much as they could get from us anyway? We support whatever bum they have down there but you give a bum a dollar every day and he'll hate you for it. You cannot buy friendship. Everybody knows that except the Government.

Everybody knows we tried to buy Castro off with foreign aid in 1960 and he turned us down flat. He knew we wouldn't do anything. What would I do? I'd go down there and explode the biggest atomic bomb we've got. Then I'd say to Castro, the next one will be a little closer, the next one closer. I think he's smart enough to get the idea and I don't think we'd have any more trouble with him. Worse thing about the whole mess is we let down the Cubans. They are good people and they are our friends. Or were. We practically invited the Commies to take them over. It might be the biggest mistake in our history.

Viet Nam is like a strike. If you don't intend to win it, don't call it.

No, I can't talk about the trials on account of the appeals. Come back next year and I'll have plenty to say. In the meantime I'll keep right on running this union as long as the members want me, and they want me, there's no question about that. If they didn't want me I wouldn't last five minutes. I'll keep right on doing what I've always done—organizing new members, trying to get better wages, hours and conditions, and a better livelihood for the individuals I represent.

This fellow sat there at the table during weeks of negotiations and took notes. He was one of the biggest businessmen in the country. He was so busy taking notes he didn't know what was going on. When we'd start discussing something he'd start shuffling paper. He'd look at his notes but he couldn't read them. I'd have to tell him where we were and what was going on. I told my kid, and he is a sharp kid, if you don't quit writing down what I say you will never learn anything. When you keep on taking notes it becomes a crutch.

War on povery? You cannot have a war on poverty with a war of words. Take West Virginia. You can put more money into that State and you'd still have more unemployment. There is only one way to get rid of poverty—supply jobs. You can do this by keeping production growth up with the population growth, recognizing and doing something about community needs, increasing pensions to keep up with the cost of living, and stopping moonlighting. A man has to have a paycheck. The Government, instead of fooling around with indirect relief, ought to put them on the payroll, right on the Government payroll. Then put them to work. There's two things they can do. In the cities pave the alleys. Do you know in Detroit, which is not a backward city, only thirty percent of the alleys are paved? Clean up your alleys and not only do you put men to work but you cut down on disease and crime. And in the country, clean out and beautify the forests. Make huge, big parks everywhere. It would be worth every dollar you spent on it.

There's no civil rights issue. It's essentially an economic problem. You show me a fellow who's drawing a good paycheck and I'll show you a fellow who doesn't want to change the country. But when he has no job and no money and no food he has a right to fight. It's all a question of those who have nothing and are entitled to it. I saw them parading around the the capitol in Lansing and they were all hungry. If I cannot eat and got no place to sleep, why not fight? How much money have we put into South America to eliminate poverty? If we cannot straighten out a little country how can we change a big one like ours? If you don't have the money to sleep in the Continental Hotel, what's the use of having the right to sleep there?

You may say that the Teamster Union is aggressive. We will not deny it. We didn't get where we are today without fighting for our rights. We will continue to do so. Maybe it is the duty of a businessman to fight against wage increases. Certainly it is my duty to fight for them. I don't see why we can't be friends in the process.

There is nothing more important to the Teamsters' Union than properous business. A depressed economy, idle plants, layoffs of workers, failure of business, hurt the members we represent, hurt their families, hurt the whole of our society. We have got to be for prosperous business, we have got to do everything we can to promote prosperity for one big reason—we are operating as a union to represent our members the best we know how. When you hear that we are putting people out of business, you cannot accept that if you understand our sense of responsibility to the people we represent.

A newspaper some months ago said in a headline: "Hoffa Says Small Business Must Go." Hoffa never said that. What Hoffa said was that in the economic picture today, small business is finding the going tough, and this is unfortunate. We have reflected long enough in these last fifteen years to recognize the truth about the state of the nation; namely that big business will get bigger. There will be less employers, and there will be a larger concentration of industrial workers, necessarily bringing about a concentration of transportation workers in America.

We are restricted by Landrum-Griffin. You got to declare any stocks you own and any business I had I got rid of so all I have is my income from the union. It is very difficult for a union man to own anything today. The Government always wants to know what stocks do I own. Do we have a contract with a company we own stocks with? How much stock do you have? They put all union fellows in with the third citizens. I could retire tomorrow morning, and, under the arrangement I have out of the pension program I have, I wouldn't have to work no more. Money has no bearing on the question. If I didn't draw a salary tomorrow morning I would continue to do what I am doing and remain president of the Teamsters' Union. If I had to get a job in the nighttime to carry on, I would do that too. Money is no big deal in my life.

I am opposed to industry-wide national strikes. But I am not opposed to a strike against an employer who is involved in multi-operations coast-to-coast that effectively cannot be struck unless it is a total company strike. There is a big difference in striking an employer nation-wide and in striking an industry nation-wide. It would take us a year to call a strike nation-wide and industry-wide, even if everybody who has a say-so approves.

To call a strike like that you gotta get a two-thirds vote and make the officers believe there is a necessity. It would be impossible to do, in my opinion. There has never been a successful nation-wide strike in Europe including in England. It's silly the way they talk about it because it just doesn't work that way.

While we sit here or walk up and down the beach. while we go home and go fishing, while we have our recreational diversions, the employer, in effect, never sleeps. While he is sleeping and while he is playing, he has departments where the whip is cracked, hours are for nought, days are for nought, until they accomplish what they are after. They hope to see the day when they will harness and control the unions of the United States and ultimately destroy their economic rights. Yes, you may say, I've heard this before, this never happened until now, yet, I say to you that it isn't true. The Employer realizes far better than you that an overdose of taking away from individuals their economic rights can be more destructive than any strike at their plants. Little by little nibbling away, little by little passing State laws, passing city regulations, federal regulations—gradually brings tremendous opportunities to the employers to be able to go into court to hamstring and destroy our organizations.

You talk about gangsters! Reporters are gangsters with a pencil instead of a gun. They distort, deceive, tell half-truths and complete lies. How do they sell newspapers except when there's something sensational on the front page? Did you ever read a headline that said there was a happily married couple that celebrated their anniversary last week? You gotta look between the obituaries and the classified ads to find stuff like that. I am not naive enough and will not accept that there is a free press in America. There are very few labor reporters in the United States that are free to write the truth about the Teamsters' Union. Most of them are controlled by the antilabor policies of their papers.

Don't get the idea that I feel like I'm being picked on. Hoffa can take care of Hoffa.

Now I regard Bobby Kennedy as a spoiled brat. He never had to work, wouldn't know how to make a living. He's just a brat that believes that everybody is supposed to surrender and give in to whatever he wants, right or wrong. In my opinion he prostitutes his oath of office, and he's violated the Constitution of the United States and is subject to go to jail. He used Government funds when he was out campaigning for legislation which is a violation of the law.

I question whether or not he has a single friend, and I question whether or not his associates are other than people who have to associate with him, and who are involved in a question of their position, or in line for some favor that he may be able to give because of his job or his wealth. As far as his associates are concerned, Bobby Kennedy should look in the mirror and find out whether or not he could stand an investigation like Hoffa has on his own personal life—and I say *personal*.

I was reading a story about Bobby Kennedy which talked about he was born to the silk and I was born to the burlap, and what the difference would have been if I had been born to the silk and Kennedy to the burlap. Well, you can't change life very easily and you can't go back, but I would venture to say that knowing what I did to get where I am now and what it took me to be part of building this union, that Bobby Kennedy would have found out that it is one thing to make people to do things and another thing to get people to do things without making them. When you are rich everybody wants to do things, favors, everything for you. When you are poor nobody wants to do a damn thing for you. That's the difference in my life, the way I came along and where I am, and his life. I know because I've had it both ways. He can't know because he never had it but one way; the rich way.

I'm willing to debate with Bobby Kennedy on radio or TV at my own personal expense, anywhere in the country, any issue he desires to debate, and then let the American people vote on whether or not they believe that the image created by Kennedy is the actual Jimmy Hoffa who is president of the International Brotherhood of Teamsters, or whether he has not used every underhanded tactic he could use, and the greatest public relations campaign in the world, to try to distort, deceive and destroy, if possible, James Hoffa. It's hard to conceive that the American people are willing to accept the theory that a young millionaire who never worked in his life, never had to face up to meeting a budget, would be able to understand, determine what is good or bad for the working people.

*   *   *   *

It is necessary to understand and recognize what we did on the West Coast, where for long numbers of years this International Union thought it was popular to fight with local unions of the Longshoremen who are called communist. When I came to this office I recognized the futility of trying to fight and pit one union against another, and I traveled to the West Coast to sit down with Harry Bridges and his organization.

We worked out an understanding where we would stop the raiding, stop the fighting and the bitterness between our unions and negotiate contracts jointly for the benefit of our rank and file. Out of the very first negotiations on the West Coast where we participated as a joint negotiating committee, we received 21c an hour, the greatest single increase they had received over the period of time we were organized.

Now we were criticized, I was criticized, very much, for making this deal with Harry Bridges, who, it was alleged by some, was a communist, but I am not so quick as some people to pass judgment on my fellow man. We recognize our responsibility to be against communists but that is the Government's responsibility before it is the Teamsters' Union's responsibility. If the Government didn't want to, couldn't find the Longshoremen or Bridges guilty do you mean to tell me it was up to the Teamster's Union to find them guilty? Our drivers drive right down to the docks and they have to work with the longshoremen they find there. It is my responsibility to get the best conditions I can get for our members. That's what I do. Now I say to you, with all that propaganda about commies in the Longshoremen, criticizing the Teamsters, I never heard anybody criticize the employers, the truckers, the railroads, the shippers, who hire the longshoremen and work with them just like we do. If the Teamsters are supposed to not cooperate with the Longshoremen, the same rule ought to apply to the employers.

And the New York Longshoremen. The papers said they were run by racketeers, racket-ridden. I don't know because that is not my responsibility. But I do know we got to do business with them because our drivers and our warehousemen deliver goods to the docks. If there is racketeering it is the police's responsibility, not our responsibility, to clean it up. Or maybe it is the employers responsibility, but nobody ever suggested that.

* * * *

Of course I voted for Johnson. No one would vote for Goldwater. You gotta be a nut to vote for him. That guy would say anything about anything. He could never back it up if he had been president. There are times to talk and times to keep your mouth shut. Goldwater never knew the difference. Anyone who is president of this country has got to have that much sense.

Anyone who is president has to be a second guesser; they are always a day late. We have to make delayed decisions because we don't control our own destiny any more.

I would have to say I think Lyndon Johnson is the best president we've had since Roosevelt; Franklin D. Roosevelt; and before his time is up he might top him. Roosevelt wanted to do the right things for the working people and he did do a lot. But he didn't have the experience and he didn't have the times with him. Johnson is a man of the people. He understands the needs of working class people because he came from that background. He has the experience of many years as a Congressman and a Senator. Look how things began to move in Congress after Johnson took over. He is smart and tough and he knows how to get along with people. That's why he could get what he wanted from Congress and still does. He can pull every beagle's ears in the country and I'm still for him.

There is no getting rid of the national debt. The end of it will be socialism. People with money are fighting a losing battle. They cannot continue on the tax structure in this country and not expect the taxation to become so great that the incentive to work will go away. I know lawyers and doctors who figure out in January how many cases they will take until the end of the year. When they reach that point they travel after that. You lose incentive.

I've got one tax case that's eight years old. I won't pay them. I know I'm right. I don't owe it to them so why should I pay it?

INDEX

179